ACT ELA in the Classroom

Bring ACT ELA prep into the classroom to enhance student learning! In this new copublication from Routledge and test-prep experts A-List Education, you'll learn how the updated ACT exam is closely aligned with the Common Core, making it easy to weave test prep into your curriculum and help students hone the skills they need for college readiness. The book is filled with practical examples of how the Common Core State Standards are connected to specific sections, question types, and strategies applicable to the ACT, so you can simultaneously prepare your students for the test while improving their reading, writing, and language skills.

Bonus: A Study Guide to help you use the book for school-wide professional development is available as a free eResource download from our website: www.routledge.com/9781138692190.

A-List Education is an educational services provider serving more than 50,000 students with tutoring programs across the U.S. as well as in the UK, Dubai, Switzerland, and China.

ACT ELA in the Classroom

Integrating Assessments, Standards, and Instruction

A-List Education

Routledge
Taylor & Francis Group
NEW YORK AND LONDON

First published 2017
by Routledge
711 Third Avenue, New York, NY 10017

and by Routledge
2 Park Square, Milton Park, Abingdon, Oxon, OX14 4RN

*Routledge is an imprint of the Taylor & Francis Group,
an informa business*

Library of Congress Cataloging-in-Publication Data
Names: A-List Education.
Title: ACT ELA in the classroom : integrating assessments, standards, and
    instruction / by A-List Education.
Description: New York : Routledge, 2017.
Identifiers: LCCN 2016011084 | ISBN 9781138692183 (hardback) |
    ISBN 9781138692190 (pbk.) | ISBN 9781315532899 (e-book)
Subjects: LCSH: ACT Assessment. | Language arts—United States. |
    Common Core State Standards (Education)
Classification: LCC LB2353.48 A45 2017 | DDC 378.1/662—dc23
LC record available at http://lccn.loc.gov/2016011084

ISBN: 978-1-138-69218-3 (hbk)
ISBN: 978-1-138-69219-0 (pbk)
ISBN: 978-1-315-53289-9 (ebk)

Typeset in Palatino
by Apex CoVantage, LLC

Printed and bound in the United States of America by Sheridan

Contents

eResources

This book is accompanied by free online eResources, including a Study Guide to help you work on this book with colleagues, as well as additional materials to help you with school-wide implementation of the ideas in this book. To access the eResources, go to www.routledge.com/9781138692190 and click on the eResources tab. Then click on the items you'd like to view. They will begin downloading to your computer.

About the Author

A-List Education was founded in 2005 with a mission to bring innovation and opportunity to education, empowering students to reach their true potential. We work with schools, school districts, families, and nonprofits and provide tailored solutions for specific learning and curriculum needs—ultimately working to improve college readiness and access. Our staff comprises experienced and passionate educators each with a distinctive and personal approach to academic success, and our management team collectively possesses 75+ years of tutoring, teaching, and test preparation experience. We now provide leading-edge education services and products to more than 500 high schools and nonprofit organizations, helping more than 70,000 students a year in the United States and around the world.

A-List has a variety of offerings for SAT and ACT preparation, including:

- **Textbooks** for students studying individually or for teachers conducting classes. Our content not only emphasizes test-taking techniques, but also reinforces core skills, which empower students for academic success long after taking the test.
- **Professional development** to help schools and organizations set up their own courses. Our seminars create valuable educational expertise that will allow teachers in your district to bring content and problem-solving strategies directly into their classrooms.
- **Direct course instruction** using our own staff. Our dedicated and experienced teachers receive intensive training before entering the classroom and have proven track records of empowering students to reach their academic potential.
- An **online portal** to remotely grade practice tests and provide supplemental material. This platform removes the burden of grading complex tests without requiring

customized technology and provides supplemental material for your ongoing courses.

◆ Individual one-on-one **tutoring**. Our instructors help students deliver average improvements of more than three times the national average in the United States. In addition, our students routinely gain acceptance to their top choice schools and have been awarded millions of dollars in scholarships.

Visit us at **www.alisteducation.com** to learn more.

Introduction and Overview

The ACT and the Common Core

The Common Core State Standards Initiative (CCSSI) is a program designed to unify the state standards across the United States so that students, parents, and educators have a clear sense of what skills students must acquire in school to become ready for college or a career. It is an independent initiative in which states may voluntarily choose to participate, but by the end of 2015, 42 states plus the District of Columbia had chosen to adopt the Standards. The Standards are designed to be rigorous, clear, and consistent, and they are based on real evidence to align with the knowledge and skill necessary for life beyond high school.

The program is controversial to be sure, but a strong foundation is already in place, and schools around the country are working to align their own materials and programs with the newly adopted standards. The Standards specifically do not outline exact requirements for curriculum, such that schools and districts can still make their own choices about how to run their classes while still adhering to the Standards. As a result, some schools may struggle to find the right material.

However, there already exists a comprehensive source of material that addresses the wide range of skills and knowledge that the Common Core emphasizes: the ACT.

Not all schools currently offer preparation programs for the ACT, but even those that do tend to treat the test as distinct from normal schoolwork. The test is seen as supplementary, and preparation is an unpleasant game in which students learn tricks to game the system without actually learning skills. This view of the test, however, is not just uncharitable, but false. In fact, ACT preparation can fill many of the gaps to help schools align their curricula with the Common Core.

The ACT requires students to use many of the same math and reading skills that are the goals of the Standards. It is designed to identify whether students are ready for college by testing them on the skills and knowledge they will need when they get there.

Preparing for the test can accomplish two goals at once. Test preparation's primary goal is to prepare for the test itself, helping students maximize their scores on the test and thus improving their chances of being admitted to the colleges of their choice. Beyond pure admissions, students' test scores can have a number of uses for different programs and institutions. For example,

- ◆ **College admissions.** Roughly half of a student's admissions profile is composed of a combination of GPA and SAT or ACT score. A high score can be a huge differentiator for the majority of elite universities, and a minimum hurdle for the majority of state universities.
- ◆ **Scholarships.** There are billions of dollars of aid in private and school-based scholarship money tied directly to test scores.
- ◆ **Community colleges.** Even at community colleges with low graduation rates, good scores can allow students to avoid placement in remedial classes.
- ◆ **Military.** For students interested in the military, baseline scores can qualify a student for officer training as opposed to regular enlistment.
- ◆ **State assessment.** The ACT is increasingly used as a statewide student assessment to identify achievement of particular benchmarks.

But test preparation is also a valuable activity in itself; students will also be working on honing and strengthening the skills they need for college readiness. Furthermore, the test material itself is valuable even beyond their application to the actual test. The passages, mathematical concepts, and other content contained herein can be divorced from the ACT. You do not have to actually take the ACT to draw value from reading and analyzing its passages, or from analyzing its grammatical structures, or from attempting to solve its math problems.

It is for these reasons that some states have decided to use the ACT as its primary measurement for high school achievement, rather than a more explicitly standards-based assessment.

Alignment

In 2010, ACT, Inc., produced an alignment study to show how the standards align with the skills that the ACT assesses. The results of this study show that the ACT significantly aligns with the standards. The ACT is constructed not according to the CCSS, but using its own College and Career Readiness Standards (CCRS). The aforementioned study aligns the CCSS to these ACT standards, not to the ACT test itself. Our purpose here is to examine this alignment in the context of real test material. It's fine to say that CCSS X aligns with ACT standard Y, but what does that mean in terms of actual test questions, the things students will actually engage with?

Since the publication of this study, the ACT has altered its ACT CCRS, but has not updated the CCSS alignment document. Most of the changes, however, should not affect alignment to CCSS. Many of the changes are cosmetic—for example, changing the wording of existing standards or re-categorizing mathematical concepts—and the test itself has not changed significantly, with the exception of the Writing section's optional essay. The essay prompt has changed format and the scoring system has changed. If anything, these changes associate the ACT CCRS more closely to the CCSS. The only substantive change that has occurred is in the Writing Test, the optional essay. The essay prompt has changed format, and the scoring system has changed.

We use the ACT's own alignment document as a starting point and elaborate based on our own extensive knowledge of and experience with test material. Interestingly, this document is no longer available on the ACT's website, possibly because the changes to their ACT CCRS make it somewhat obsolete. It is still possible to find it online hosted elsewhere with a bit of searching.

In short, the ACT was already very strongly aligned to the CCSS before they changed their standards. Since then, the test has changed very little, and their standards have moved *closer* to the CCSS.

(Interestingly, this document is no longer available on the ACT's website, possibly because the changes to their ACT CCRS make it somewhat obsolete. It is still possible to find it hosted elsewhere with a bit of searching.)

About This Book

This book has two main goals:

1. To show how specific ACT English, Reading, and Writing material aligns with the ELA CCSS.
2. To discuss how to incorporate ACT preparation into your regular English classes outside of an explicit test preparation class.

Why do we focus on the CCSS? First of all, because the grand majority of states use it. There's no shortage of debate about the value of the standards, but it's undeniable that they are in place throughout most of the country. Even some states that are moving away from the standards are doing so more in name than in practice and are keeping the content of the CCSS in place.

Of course, not every state uses CCSS, but it remains a useful framework for connecting ACT material to classroom material. We can't run through every state's particulars in one book, but the popularity of the CCSS makes them a convenient reference. If you don't use them, you can still use CCSS as a touchstone to compare to your own state standards. Even if you do use CCSS, your state may also have its own assessments or graduation requirements that deviate from CCSS. The alignment information is one piece of the picture.

Second, some states are actually using the ACT as their main statewide assessment. They are generally doing so because of the ACT's alignment to the Common Core. Is this a good idea? That's debatable, and we won't take sides here. The question is part political, part pedagogical, often emotional. However, we can offer our research and expertise in the test so you can help see for yourself where it coincides with your curriculum and where it doesn't.

Structure of the Book

Part I will describe the structure and content of the ACT's ELA sections for those who may be unfamiliar with the test, along with some effective test-taking techniques. Keep in mind that this is a general overview. It draws information from our main textbook, *The Book of Knowledge*, which is the product of years of experience with the test and goes into much greater detail about the test's content and the most effective strategies.

Part II will connect the ACT to the Common Core ELA standards (Reading, Writing, and Language). This section will take a closer look at showing where the test does and does not align with these Standards. It will go through each individual standard one by one to discuss what specific sections, question types, or strategies align with the standard in question. Additional discussion also describes how, even when the test does not align with the standard, test material can be pushed beyond its intended scope in order to do so.

Parts III and IV will focus on how to use all this material in the classroom. This could mean using your classes as explicit preparation for the test; it could mean using test material to supplement your regular classes; it could mean preparing for the test as a tool with which to get your students to meet the standards; or it could be a combination of these things. This section will include some discussions and samples to help get you started.

The Appendices will list all of the alignment tables discussed in Part II as well as a bibliography and suggestions for further reading.

1

About the ACT

In recent years, the ACT has made an active effort to emphasize college readiness benchmarks to a greater degree than they did before. They have introduced ACT Aspire, a suite of assessment for students starting as early as third grade, using a longitudinal assessment of benchmarks into high school. They are moving past the market of individual students taking the test for college and marketing their tests directly to schools, to be used both for college admissions and for skills assessment.

Is this a good idea? Who knows? There's certainly a great deal of debate about the value of assessments in general, let alone this particular test. But in the meantime, it's here, so we must acknowledge it and deal with it. The test has been relatively unchanged for several decades (with a few exceptions we'll discuss soon), so we do know quite a bit about what's on the test and have years of experience preparing students for it.

We want to help you incorporate ACT material into your classroom in order to prepare students without running an explicit ACT prep course. To do so, the first and most important thing is simply to know what's on the test and what the test is like. The best way to do that is firsthand: *You should absolutely do some official practice tests yourself.* There is a full-length practice test available for free download on the ACT's website. Go do one and see what you think.

In the meantime, we're not going to go through our whole prep book (but it is for sale on our website!), but we do want to give you an overview of the structure and content of the test.

Format

The ACT is composed of four sections (called "tests"), plus an optional fifth, always presented in this order:

Test	Number of Questions	Time	Description
English	75	45 minutes	Multiple-choice grammar and usage questions.
Math	60	60 minutes	Multiple-choice math questions.
Reading	40	35 minutes	Multiple-choice reading comprehension questions.
Science	40	35 minutes	Multiple-choice data interpretation questions
Writing	*1 essay*	*40 minutes*	*Optional. One 1- to 4-page essay.*
Total	**215**	**2 hours 55 minutes**	
with essay	*215 + essay*	*3 hours 35 minutes*	

Most multiple-choice questions have four choices, except for questions on the Math Test, which have five choices. The letters of the answer choices alternate ABCD/FGHJ every other question. On the Math Test, the five choices alternate ABCDE/FGHJK.

The ACT does not take off points for wrong answers. This means that random guessing will not count against you. A wrong answer counts the same as a blank.

Students will get a score from 1 to 36 on each of the four main tests, plus a Composite score, which is the *average* of the four test scores—English, Math, Reading, and Science—rounded to the nearest whole number.

Everyone will also get a STEM score, which is just the rounded average of your Math and Science scores. This score will *not* be included in your Composite score.

Students who choose to take the Writing section (the essay) will get additional scores:

- Four subscores from 2 to 12 in different aspects of your essay
- A final Writing score from 2 to 12 that is the rounded average of the four subscores. This is a change, starting with the September 2016 test. In the 2015–2016 school year, students receive a scaled writing score on the 1 to 36 point scale.

When the Writing score was a scaled 36-point score, students who took Writing also received an ELA score on the 36-point scale, which was the rounded average of the English, Reading, and Writing scores. While the Writing score will no longer be on that scale, the ACT said the ELA score will continue to be reported. However, as of this printing, the ACT has not announced how the ELA score will be calculated.

ACT scores are calculated by taking the number of right answers (the "raw score"), and translating that score into a final score using a special scoring table. Each test has its own unique scoring table in order to adjust for slight difficulty differences among tests. The national average Composite score is generally around 21, but average scores can vary by state and by component test.

For a detailed look at test format, ACT, Inc., publishes a book called *The Official ACT Prep Guide 2016–2017*, which contains three official full-length tests.

Recent Changes

The ACT has not undergone any radical changes like the SAT has. However, in the past few years, there have been a few changes that may be noticeable.

- ◆ The essay format and scoring system has radically changed as of September 2015. The old essay featured a different kind of prompt and each essay grader gave each essay only one 1- to 6-point score. The STEM and ELA scores are also new additions.
- ◆ Starting in 2014, one of the four passages on the Reading Test will now be a double passage, with two different passages on a similar topic and one set of questions about them.
- ◆ The distribution of passage types has changed slightly on the Science Tests. Previously the test always contained seven passages, each with five to seven questions, following strict rules about number of questions per passages. As of 2015, some tests have had only six passages with more fluidity in the number of questions per passage, and future tests may have six or seven passages.
- ◆ The Math Test had a similar change in the distribution of question types. However, the change in Math is subtle so few people would notice it unless they were looking closely.

If you are using practice tests published before 2015, such as the older book, *The Real ACT Prep Guide 3rd Edition*, the tests will *not* reflect these changes. For the most part that's fine; a seven-passage Science Test isn't significantly different from a six-passage Science Test. The essay change is significant—you shouldn't waste time doing essays in the old format—but the essay is optional, so you can always skip it entirely if doing an older test. Their most recent book, *The Official ACT Prep Guide 2016–2017*, does contain new-format tests, as does the current test that's available for free download on actstudent.org (form 1572CPRE).

This book will focus on the ACT English, Reading, and Writing Tests. We will not be discussing the Math or Science Tests.

English

The English test is composed of five short passages, each of which has 15 questions that ask about the grammar, usage, style, and rhetoric of the passage. English questions fall into two main categories: *Usage and Mechanics* (40 questions) and *Rhetorical Skills* (35 questions).

Usage/Mechanics

Usage/Mechanics questions ask students to identify errors in a sentence. Generally, a word or part of a sentence will be underlined, and they will be asked to choose how to rewrite the phrase according to rules of grammar, usage, and punctuation. Choice A or F will usually be "NO CHANGE", meaning they can leave the phrase as it was originally written.

There are three types of Usage/Mechanics questions:

◆ **Grammar and Usage.** These questions test relationships between single words and phrases within a sentence, relationships such as subject and verb, or pronoun and antecedent.

◆ **Sentence Structure.** These questions deal with the way larger parts of sentences are connected, such as the way to properly connect clauses and where to place long phrases.

◆ **Punctuation.** These questions will usually present four choices that differ *only* in their punctuation. Students will be tested on when to use (and when not to use) commas, apostrophes, and other common punctuation marks.

Rhetorical Skills

Rhetorical Skills Questions focuses less on writing *grammatically* and more on writing *effectively*. It tests how to choose the best way to phrase a sentence, the best way to structure a paragraph, or the best way to accomplish the writer's goal. Unlike Usage/Mechanics Questions, Rhetorical Skills Questions may ask about the essay as a whole, not just single words or phrases.

There are three types of Rhetorical Skills Questions:

◆ **Style.** These questions ask about the choice of language in the essay, as well as stylistic errors rather than grammatical or structural ones. Students will be asked to trim wordy sentences, make phrases more specific, or ensure the language accurately reflects the essay's tone.

◆ **Organization.** These questions ask about the logic and organization of the essay. Students will be asked about the location and ordering of sentences and the transitions between sentences or paragraphs.

◆ **Writing Strategy.** These questions ask about what the author should do to the essay to improve it. In fact, most Writing Strategy Questions will explicitly phrase the question that way, asking what action the author should take. Common questions include whether the author should add or delete a sentence and whether the essay fulfills a certain goal.

Reading

The Reading Test is composed of four passages, each of which has ten questions that ask about the content of the passages, inferences or conclusions that can be drawn from the passages, or the author's rhetorical strategies. All questions on the Reading Test are multiple-choice passage-based questions with four possible choices.

The four passages will be in the following topics: *Prose Fiction*, *Social Science*, *Humanities*, and *Natural Science*. They will always be in that order, and the passage will state which type it is, as well as the source of the passage. One of the passages will be a *double passage*, in which two passages on a similar topic are presented, followed by questions discussing each passage individually or the relationship between the two.

A few idiosyncrasies about the ACT Reading to keep in mind:

◆ ACT Reading questions will not be in any particular order at all. They are not in order of difficulty nor in chronological order of events in the passage. The question order will be random.

◆ ACT questions do not always provide line references directing students to the specific place in the passage where the answer can be found.

◆ The timing is very tight. Students often have trouble finishing the ACT Reading Test.

Strategies

Main Ideas
One of the biggest problems students have with the passages is that reading takes a long time. Students try to memorize every point and understand every subtle detail and convoluted sentence in the passage. Instead, read the passage quickly and get the *main ideas*. Every paragraph is nothing more than a collection of sentences that have some common theme. That common theme is the main idea of the paragraph. It's the answer to this question: *What's it about?*

The goal is to *spend less time reading the passage* so you can spend *more time on the questions*, since the questions are what actually matter. Therefore, when reading the passage, skim the details and focus on the overall themes. These themes should be simple: the plot of the story, the argument of the essay, or the description of the information given. The details will become important only when and if a question asks about them.

Go Back to the Passage

Sometimes questions will give a line reference saying exactly where in the passage the relevant information can be found. Once students read the question, before doing anything else, they should *go back to the passage and check the line reference*. If a question asks about line 35, go back to line 35 and see what it says before looking at the choices.

While students should not worry about the details when reading the passage, they can worry about the details once questions actually ask about them. The point is not to rely on what you remember about the passage. This is an open-book test. You can look it up.

Anticipate

All the information you need is in the passage itself. Read the question, follow the line reference back into the passage, and see what those lines say about the question. That's your *anticipation* of the answer to the question. Try to *paraphrase* the lines in your own word. The right answer will rarely be an *exact* match for the anticipation; rather, the right answer will have the same *meaning* as the anticipation, but worded differently. Then look at the choices and see which one matches the anticipation.

Eliminate

Sometimes it will be difficult to anticipate the answer based on the passage alone, but you can still eliminate choices that are obviously wrong and guess from what's left. Wrong choices are usually wrong for one of three reasons:

- ◆ **Random.** The choice talks about things that the passage doesn't even mention.
- ◆ **False.** The choice is explicitly contradicted by the passage.
- ◆ **Irrelevant.** The choice is something the author *says*, but it doesn't actually answer the question.

Note that all three of these reasons require you to have an understanding of what the passage does and doesn't say. But seeing that a wrong choice is wrong is often simpler that understanding the nuances of the correct answer. It's easier to spot a wrong choice than a right choice—after all, 75% of the choices are wrong.

Question Types

The Book of Knowledge categorizes ACT Reading questions into the following question types based on those defined by the makers of the ACT.

Explicit Questions

These are the questions that ask what the passage literally says. Go back, anticipate the answer, and then match that anticipation to the choices. Explicit Questions are the most common question type on the ACT: over a third of all reading questions are explicit. They appear throughout the test, but they are somewhat more common on Social Studies/Sciences passages than on Arts/Literature passages.

ACT Explicit Questions rarely have line references—fewer than one in five do. But the good news is that once students do find the information in the passage, the right answer often matches the wording of the passage very closely.

Inferential Questions

Rather than asking about what is literally in the passage, these questions ask students to make conclusions and inferences based on the information in the passage. Inferential Questions are the second most common question type, making up about a fifth of the questions.

It may sound like Inferential Questions are harder than Explicit Questions, but that's not always the case. Inferential Questions can sometimes be quite easy. Sometimes a question will *technically* require an inference—the passage doesn't *literally* say the correct answer—but the information stated in the passage is so close to the correct choice that it's virtually explicit.

Main Idea Questions

Main Idea Questions ask for the main idea of a paragraph, a group of paragraphs, or the entire passage. These questions might also ask for the central "function", "theme", "conflict", or "purpose" of a paragraph. They will usually give a specific reference to which paragraph or paragraphs they are asking about.

Generalization Questions

Generalization Questions ask students to make a short generalization about a large amount of information in the passage. They are more common on Arts/Literature passages than Social Studies/Sciences passages.

Generalization Questions are similar to Main Idea Questions in that they ask about large sections of the passage. But they don't necessarily point to specific paragraphs or sections of the passage. Rather they're about themes and ideas that run throughout. Therefore, the answer to these questions may not be in a single place, and the questions rarely give line references. Generalization Questions may also ask about the tone, opinions, beliefs, or attitudes of any character in the passage.

Meaning Questions

These questions ask students to identify the meaning of a word, phrase, or sentence in the passage. It may be the literal meaning of the sentence in the context of a larger argument. Or it may ask for the figurative or metaphorical meaning of the sentence. Meaning Questions almost always give a line reference, so students will know exactly where to look.

Meaning Questions are similar to Explicit Questions, but they require an additional level of interpretations. Explicit Questions ask "what does the author say?" or "when the author says X, what does X *refer* to?" Meaning Questions, however, ask "when the author says X, what does he *mean* by X?" This may require an inference, it may require knowledge of the main idea, or it may just require that you look in the line above or below. *Vocabulary-in-Context Questions* are a subcategory of Meaning Questions. They work exactly the same way, but ask about a single word.

Strategy Questions

Strategy Questions ask about the author's intentions or techniques. These questions could ask about the literal structure of the passage, its organization, the author's motivation for presenting information in a certain way, or why the author uses a particular rhetorical strategy. Any "meta" question, or question that asks about the *form* of the passage instead of its *content*, can be classified as a Strategy Question.

Writing

Format

The Writing Test consists of one 40-minute essay, always the last section of the test. The Writing Test is optional, but some colleges do require it, particularly top-tier schools.

The essay will be read by two readers, each giving the essay a score from 1 to 6 in four domains: Ideas and Analysis, Development and Support, Organization, and Language. The readers' scores are added together to make the subscores in each domain, on a 2 to 12 point scale. The final Writing score is the rounded average of these four subscores. Essays that are blank, illegible, or off topic will receive no score, and no Writing or ELA scores will be reported.

The essay will be evaluated in the following four domains:

- **Ideas and Analysis.** Do you address all three of the perspectives given? Do you understand the purpose of the essay? Do you take a clear position on the topic question? Do you offer context?
- **Development and Support.** Do you develop your ideas? Do you elaborate on your ideas?
- **Organization.** Is your essay well organized? Are your paragraphs related by a main idea? Are your transitions logical? Are your introduction and conclusion effective?
- **Language.** Do you show competent command of language? Do you show varied sentence structure? Do you make distracting errors?

Topic

Students may write up to four pages on the given topic. The topics are generally broad enough that students won't need any specific knowledge. The ACT essay is framed as a *persuasive* essay, not a *descriptive* essay. Students will need to actively argue a position, making it more like a debate topic than an English Literature essay.

The essay prompt will have several parts to it. There will be an introduction that outlines the context of the issue, and *three contrasting perspectives* on the issue. Immediately beneath these perspectives you'll find the essay task instructions and some advice on planning the essay. The essay task and instructions will always be the same, with only minor changes to the question in the task.

Here is a sample essay prompt from *The Book of Knowledge*:

Genetic Screening

It is now possible through genetic testing to determine an individual's likelihood of developing several different kinds of diseases, some of them debilitating or fatal. With such knowledge it may be possible for some people to seek early treatment or adopt lifestyle changes that may prevent or ameliorate these diseases. But others have no cure and no treatment or change in lifestyle will help. How much should we and do we want to know about our genetic disposition to disease? Should doctors tell patients? Who should have access to such information?

Read and carefully consider these perspectives. Each suggests a particular way of thinking about the issue of genetic screening for disease.

Perspective 1	Perspective 2	Perspective 3
The more we know about ourselves, the better. Even if we learn that we will eventually develop a fatal disease, we deserve to know that and live our lives accordingly.	No science is exact, certainly not genetic testing. The possibility of inaccurate results is high. A false positive could destroy the life of a healthy person.	Our greatest concern should be individual privacy. It's easy to talk about doctor–patient confidentiality, but it is impossible to guarantee complete privacy.

Essay Task

Write a unified, coherent essay in which you evaluate multiple perspectives on the issue of genetic screening for disease. In your essay, be sure to:

◆ Analyze and evaluate the perspectives given
◆ State and develop your own perspective on the issue
◆ Explain the relationship between your perspective and those given

Your perspective may be in full agreement with any of the others, in partial agreement, or wholly different. Whatever the case, support your ideas with logical reasoning and detailed, persuasive examples.

Strategies

The ACT essay does not require any specific outside knowledge; the topic should be something easily understandable, and most of the necessary information will be given in the prompt. However, the topic is very specific, and students may have trouble coming up with specific examples beyond what is described in the prompt.

On the essay, students must engage with the multiple given perspectives on a topic of general contemporary interest. There's no one single way that you have to proceed in order to get a good score, but in general, the more nuanced your take is, the better you'll do.

Whether or not the student's thesis agrees with any of the perspectives, they must present some support or evidence that relates to each of the three perspectives. Students should try to come up with a few reasons or examples to support each perspective before they start writing. This doesn't have to be elaborate; just jot down a few ideas.

The easiest way to proceed is to simply argue in favor of one of the given perspectives. Students should choose to support the perspective for which they can come up with the most supporting evidence, regardless of whether that perspective is their actual opinion. The topic already gives a few reasons within each perspective, which can be a good starting point, but students must go beyond them in order to get a good score. In order to get a top score, students will want to go beyond the stated perspectives and come up with their own original thesis on the topic. Discussing possible reasons and examples for the perspectives given in sample topics is an excellent and productive classroom activity.

Before writing, students should practice outlining and organizing their essays. Students should explicitly state their thesis, whether it is in complete agreement with one of the given perspectives or a different take on the topic altogether. Paragraphs should be organized into discrete, coherent topics. Most students should write three body paragraphs, each one addressing each perspective and how that perspective agrees or disagrees with their thesis. For perspectives that do not align with the thesis, it is important for students to give examples and reasoning for why those perspectives are flawed.

Finally, practice essays should be reviewed together so students can begin to get a concrete sense of what effective and ineffective writing look like. Workshopping topics and examples, re-reading past essays, and making revisions are all beyond the scope of a 40-minute essay, but they can help build the writing skills that students will need.

ACT vs. SAT

With the recent redesign to the SAT beginning in 2016, many users of the old SAT have been looking to move to the ACT instead. The redesigned SAT is actually much more similar to the ACT than the old SAT was. Let's take a quick look at the differences between the tests.

Section	ACT	SAT	Content Differences
English (called "Writing" on SAT)	75 questions 45 minutes 0.6 min/q	44 questions 35 minutes 0.8 min/q	Content between the two tests is virtually identical. SAT has some passages that have accompanying tables or figures.
Math	60 questions 60 minutes 1 min/q	58 questions 80 minutes 1.4 min/q	Math concepts are mostly the same. The SAT • has a no-calculator section • has two sections • has less geometry, more statistics • has some non-multiple-choice questions
Reading	40 questions 35 minutes 0.88 min/q	52 questions 65 minutes 1.25 min/q	Question types are mostly the same. The SAT • has passages that come with tables or figures • explicitly asks to find evidence • does not have a Humanities passage • has some older primary source passages
Science	40 questions 35 min 0.88 min/q	None	No Science section on SAT. Data figures on Reading and Writing passages involve similar concepts.
Writing (called "Essay" on SAT)	40 minutes	50 minutes	SAT essay prompt is based on reading and analyzing a given passage.

◆ The biggest difference is in timing. Students have less time per question on the ACT. Students who have particular problems with timing should seriously consider taking the SAT.

- The most noticeable content difference is that the SAT does not have a Science section. However, SAT Reading and Writing sections contain some questions about interpreting tables and graphs in a context, questions that require similar skills as the ACT Science Test.

- The Math sections show the biggest difference in format. The SAT splits its math across two different sections, instead of one big section on the ACT. On one of those sections, calculators are not permitted, while they are permitted on all math questions on the ACT. And each of the two SAT Math sections contain some "Grid-In" Questions for which students must provide their own answers, whereas all ACT questions are multiple choice.

- However, the two Math Tests use very similar math content. The biggest difference is the distribution of concepts. The SAT has much less geometry, less than 10% of the questions on the SAT, and much more statistics and data analysis, about 30%.

- The Reading and Writing content are also very similar between the two tests. The Writing in particular is shockingly identical.

- The essay prompts are in very different formats, but both tests' essays are optional.

2

Alignment with Common Core ELA Standards

How to Read the ELA Standards

The ELA standards are divided into strands (Reading, Writing, Speaking and Listening, Language). Each strand has a list of College and Career Readiness (CCR) Anchor Standards. These are the broad standards that students must attain in order to be deemed fit for college or a career beyond high school.

In addition, these standards are broken out for each grade level from kindergarten to grade 12, outlining what a student must be able to do and understand by the end of that grade level. For high school, standards are shown for two groupings, grades 9–10 and grades 11–12. Some grade-specific standards are further broken down into multiple subskills.

Some of these strands are also broken out into different content areas. For example, Reading has one set of Anchor Standards, but has different grade-level standards for Reading Literature and Reading Informational Texts.

Each standard has a code containing three parts: letters denoting the strand or content area, the grade level of the standard or "CCR" for Anchor Standards, and the sequential number of the standard (sometimes with letters for subpoints). For example, "RL.CCR.5" refers to the fifth Anchor Standard in the Reading Literature strand, and "W.11-12.3a" refers to the first subskill of the third standard for the grade 11–12 standards in the Writing strand.

Alignment

How Was Alignment Determined?

To determine alignment, we started with the ACT, Inc.'s own 2010 study aligning the ACT Standards to the CCSS. From there, we elaborated in order to contextualize to test content and made adjustments according to how the test has changed.

The following chart outlines the results for ELA standards, showing what percent of the standards in each strand align with the ACT's stated skill set.

Common Core State Standard	ACT Alignment
READING	
Reading Anchor Standards [R]	100%
Reading Standards for Literature (11-12) [RL]	67%
Reading Standards for Informational Text (11-12) [RI]	60%
WRITING	
Writing Anchor Standards [W]	50%
Writing Standards (11-12)	50%
LANGUAGE	
Language Anchor Standards [L]	100%
Language Standards (11-12)	100%
Language Progressive Skills	100%
Language Standards (11-12) and Progressive Skills	100%
SPECIAL TOPICS	
Reading for Literacy in History/Social Studies [RH]	30%
Reading for Literacy in Science and Technical Subjects [RST]	100%
Writing for Literacy in History/Social Studies, Science and Technical Subjects [WHST]	11%
Speaking and Listening [SL]	0%

Note that this table, based on the ACT's own alignment document, only considers primary standards, not the associated subskills. So if a standard aligns, but its two grade-level subskills do not, the ACT considers it aligned. This is most noticeably odd for the Language Standards (11-12): the test is aligned with 100% of the standards, but only 62% of the standards plus subskills.

The actual alignments performed were for a larger suite of materials than just the ACT. The ACT, Inc. offers additional tests and programs besides the main college admissions tests. At the time, the alignment document was produced, these included EXPLORE and PLAN, given to students earlier in high school (these tests have since been discontinued and replaced with the PreACT). Each test was aligned against the standards for the grade level the particular program is meant to be given. This document will focus on alignment for the ACT Test itself, which was aligned to the Standards for Reading, Writing, and Language for high school.

Some standards show what we call "partial alignment". In the ACT alignment report, the portion of the standard that is aligned with the ACT was highlighted in yellow. If part but not all of a standard aligned with the ACT, only those parts that align were highlighted. The table shows percentages of standards that show any alignment; it does not distinguish partial and complete alignment.

For more information about how alignment was determined, please refer to the study itself, which is listed in the bibliography at the end of this document.

How to Read This Section

The section is divided into four parts relating to the strands of the ELA standards:

- **Reading.** Ten Anchor Standards, with grade-specific standards in Literature and Informational Texts.
- **Writing.** Ten Anchor Standards, with grade-specific standards and multiple subskills.
- **Language.** Six Anchor Standards with grade-specific standards and multiple subskills. This section also reviews the Language Progressive Skills.
- **Special topics.** These topics are not discussed in detail because they are less directly relevant for ACT work.

Each section addresses each Anchor Standard together with all its associated grade-specific standard for grades 11–12. Standards within each strand are usually organized into three or four groups of related concepts. (Please note that the headings listed for those groups come from the standards themselves, while the headings for the individual standards were written by A-List.)

The discussion of each standard is composed of several parts:

Table
Each Anchor Standard is shown in a table followed by the grade-specific standard for grades 11–12. Each table contains columns showing:

- The code for the standard, as defined by the CCSSI
- The standard itself
- Its alignment with the ACT

The two alignment columns will each display one of the following symbols:

- **Y** = The standard is aligned with the ACT.
- **N** = The standard is not aligned with the ACT.
- **P** = The standard is partially aligned with the ACT.

If the standard aligns with a different subject than one would expect, or with more than one subject of the test, then the letter of that subject will also be listed. For example, if a Reading standard aligns with an ACT Science Skill, "YS" will be listed in the alignment column.

Alignment

Following the tables, we will briefly summarize the alignment with the CCR Anchor Standards and any grade-specific standards. If a standard is partially aligned—that is, the document considered it aligned, but with a qualification, or it only considered a portion of the standard to be aligned—we will list here which segments do and do not.

Discussion

Here we discuss why and how the standards align and don't align. For those that don't align well with the test itself, we discuss how the standards might align to the skills and techniques used during the act of preparation. Furthermore, we discuss ways to incorporate material from the test into tasks beyond the scope of the test. Note the original alignment document often does not give detailed explanations about why a standard does or does not align with the test. Any discussion of such here is our own judgment based on our extensive experience and knowledge of the ACT.

Summary

We give a summary of the previous discussion. This summary may also list suggestions for how to use test material in ways beyond the test's scope in order to meet a standard that otherwise does not align.

Sample ACT Questions

When a domain contains standards that align with the test, we provide some sample questions that demonstrate the concepts from the standards in that domain. All sample questions come from the ACT's book *The Official ACT Prep Guide 2016–2017* that demonstrate the key concepts. All problems are listed with a three-number code, defining as

[test number].[section number].[question number]

Thus "1.3.15" is test 1, section 3, question 15 in the book. Section 1 is always the English Test; it contains 75 questions. Section 3 is always the Reading Test; it contains 40 questions.

Three Levels of Alignment

Whether or not a standard aligns with the ACT is not always a simple question. There are three levels of alignment discussed in this document:

1. **Skills directly assessed by the test.** This is the substance of the alignment document prepared by the ACT, Inc. itself. The test already has its own list of skills that it measures directly. The skills needed for a student to meet each standard were compared to the skills students directly use when completing the test.

2. **Skills that are not assessed but are directly relevant.** These skills are not strictly necessary to answer the test *questions*, but they still are relevant to the act of test *preparation*. For example, Writing standard 5 says students should revise their writing, but the ACT essay does not give students enough time to significantly revise their essays. However, in order to improve performance, it is vital that students review their essays after the test and figure out how it could have been better. Revision is a perfect way to do so.

3. **Skills that are beyond the scope of the test as written.** These skills clearly do not apply to the ACT. For example, several skills mention using technology or outside sources, both of which are not permitted on the ELA sections. However, teachers can still use and adapt the test material for larger assignments and projects that do align with these standards.

Alignment Beyond the Test

The amount of alignment relevant to you depends on your goal for your class. If you are simply teaching test preparation for the sake of doing well on the tests, you should be concerned with the skills that are required to answer the questions and the skills that will be needed during the test-prep classroom activities. These skills alone account for the majority of the standards. This is an important point; you can be confident that *test prep is fully compatible with the Common Core* and helps students acquire and refine real skills they will need and use in college or careers.

Third-level alignment will not be relevant to test preparation, but test material needn't just be used for test preparation. These tests are a fertile raw material that can be adapted to fit your goals in your regular classes as well. For example, if you want to work on writing persuasive essays, you can use practice ACT prompts to get started. These prompts have certain time, space, and other restrictions when given on the ACT, but you can use them in your classes however you wish, including for group collaboration, graphic or multimedia displays, or extensive research. If you are working to build reading comprehension skills for informative texts, but you don't have a ready supply of nonfiction texts, any practice ACT will have many nonfiction passages you can use to get started. Don't think of these tests as just tests; they are your own academic playgrounds.

Remember also that some standards will align poorly. The test will not perfectly satisfy all the Common Core requirements. Test preparation should not replace your usual English classes, but it can *supplement* them. Test prep gives you more reading drills, more writing exercises, more resources for grammatical instruction, all of it fully compatible with the standards. Not every standard aligns with the test, but every question on the test aligns with the standards.

Reading

Overview

The Reading strand is divided into four different content areas: Standards for Literature (RL), Standards for Informational Text (RI), Standards for Literacy in History/Social Studies (RH), and Standards for Literacy in Science and Technical Subjects (RST). All of these areas are tied to the same set of CCR Anchor Standards, but each has its own separate set of grade-specific standards (though many of these are similar to each other). The standards for History/Social Studies and Science and Technical Subjects are not considered to be a part of the English Language Arts Standards, so those will be discussed in a separate section.

There are ten CCR Anchor Standards for Reading. These are organized into four groups of similar concepts. Each section below lists the Anchor Standard followed by the grade-specific standard for grades 11–12 in Reading Literature and Reading Informational Text.

Each standard in this section is aligned against the ACT's Reading section, unless otherwise marked.

Here are a few notes about Reading before we get into the specifics:

♦ All of the Reading CCR Anchor Standards align with the ACT. The majority of the grade-specific standards in both Reading for Literature and Reading for Informational Texts align with the test. If you spend time preparing for the ACT, you can be confident you are helping students acquire and refine real skills they will need and use in college or careers.

♦ The ACT's passages use four content areas: Literary Narrative/Prose Fiction, Social Science/Social Studies, Humanities, and Natural Science. Generally speaking, the first area aligns with the Reading for Literature standards, while the other three align with the Informational Text standards. However, some of the nonfiction passages may still be "literature".

♦ There will be no poetry or drama on the ACT. That means that there will be no passages from Shakespeare. Any standards that specifically ask students to study Shakespeare are outside the scope of the tests.

♦ Social Studies passages may be about historical or historiographical topics, but they generally will not be primary historical texts. That means that there will be no passages taken from original American Foundational documents. There may be passages that talk *about* these texts, but no outside knowledge would be needed. Any standards that specifically ask students to study foundational documents are outside the scope of the test.

◆ Remember that these passages do not have to be used just for test prep. Any book of practice tests contains a virtual library of short passages on a wide variety of topics. You can have your students read them without the questions; you can make up your own questions; you give a mini passage as a pop quiz if you have a few spare minutes in class; you can look up the source of a passage and read a larger section of the original text. (The test lists the source at the beginning of each passage.) If you are doing serious test prep, you have to follow the test's rules, but if you're not, you can use the passages however you like. Be creative.

Key Ideas and Details

1. Read Closely

Code	Standard	Aligns
R.CCR.1	**Read closely to determine what the text says explicitly and to make logical inferences from it; cite specific textual evidence when writing or speaking to support conclusions drawn from the text.**	**P**
RL.11-12.1	Cite strong and thorough textual evidence to support analysis of what the text says explicitly as well as inferences drawn from the text, including determining where the text leaves matters uncertain.	**N**
RI.11-12.1	Cite strong and thorough textual evidence to support analysis of what the text says explicitly as well as inferences drawn from the text, including determining where the text leaves matters uncertain.	**N**

Alignment

The ACT is aligned with only to the first half of the CCR Anchor, "Read closely to determine what the text says explicitly and to make logical inferences." It is not aligned with the second half of the CCR or the two grade-specific standards.

Discussion

What Aligns
The first part of the CCR Anchor matches perfectly with a primary goal of both tests' reading passages. For the ACT, the most common question types ask students to find information explicitly stated by the passage or make inferences based on material stated by the passage. This is the essence of reading passages.

This standard perfectly describes two of the most common types of questions that together make up over half of the Reading section. *Explicit Questions* ask students to find information that is explicitly stated in the passage. *Inferential Questions* ask students to make inferences based on material stated in the passage.

What Doesn't Align

The reason that these standards are only partially aligned is that the ACT itself does not require students to literally *cite* evidence for their responses. This is simply a multiple-choice test; all that matters to the test is the correct answer, not the students' reasoning.

However, it's virtually impossible to discuss any of this material without backing up conclusions with evidence. All our strategies for reading passages heavily rely on finding concrete evidence. Remember that these passages do not require any outside content knowledge other than vocabulary. That means all the needed information is right there in the passage. For every question, there is concrete evidence in the passage to support the correct choice.

The first rule of every passage question is to go back to the passage and find the information related to the question. The ACT does not always give line references, so it can be difficult to find the necessary information. But that just means that preparing for the ACT is good training for this skill; it forces students to do more work in order to justify their answers. Even in cases when the students cannot anticipate the answer simply by going back to the passage, they should be able to cite evidence to refute and eliminate the incorrect choices.

Summary

Alignment

Many, if not most, reading questions on the ACT ask students to determine what a text explicitly says or to make inferences based on the text.

Beyond Alignment

While the test itself does not require students to cite specific evidence, it is crucial that students use evidence from the passages or sentences when choosing their answers. As teachers, you can and should demand that students justify all their choices with cited evidence.

Sample ACT Questions

Explicit Questions: 1.3.5, 1.3.16, 2.3.12, 2.3.23, 3.3.30, 3.3.40

Inferential Questions: 1.3.9, 1.3.22, 2.3.16, 2.3.35, 3.3.7, 3.3.24

2. Central Ideas or Themes

Code	Standard	Aligns
R.CCR.2	**Determine central ideas or themes of a text and analyze their development; summarize the key supporting details and ideas.**	**Y**
RL.11-12.2	Determine two or more themes or central ideas of a text and analyze their development over the course of the text, including how they interact and build on one another to produce a complex account; provide an objective summary of the text.	**P**
RI.11-12.2	Determine two or more central ideas of a text and analyze their development over the course of the text, including how they interact and build on one another to provide a complex analysis; provide an objective summary of the text.	**P**

Alignment

The ACT is completely aligned with the CCR Anchor. It is aligned with the two grade-specific standards with the exception of the phrase "two or more".

Discussion

What Aligns

This standard directly addresses A-List's *Main Idea Strategy*. Because of time constraints, students will not have enough time to read a passage as carefully as they might on their own. That's not to say that students won't need to understand nuances of a passage, just that they shouldn't look for them right away. As we saw in the discussion of standard 1, they can find details by going back to the passage when a question asks about them, not before.

However, that doesn't mean they should ignore the passage entirely and jump right to the questions. On the contrary, it is important for them to have a sense of the overall story, information, or argument presented in the passage. Therefore, when students first encounter a passage, they should read the passage quickly, finding only the main ideas of each paragraph and of the passage as a whole.

There are several benefits to the Main Idea Strategy beyond simple time management. First, by physically writing main ideas of each paragraph in the margins, students effectively produce a kind of outline of the passage. This will make it easier to find specific details if specific line references aren't given in a question.

Additionally, it helps focus their understanding of the progression of themes in the passage, which gives them a deeper understanding of the passage itself. Questions will often explicitly ask students for the main idea of a paragraph or the passage. Other times, knowledge of main ideas can help eliminate choices quickly. As we saw above, Main Idea Questions was one of the primary question types for the ACT.

The importance of main ideas is particularly evident for double passages on the ACT. Double passages will present two passages on similar or overlapping themes. Understanding the connection between the two author's arguments or perspectives is often crucial to double-passage questions. The relationship between the passages may be as simple as the pro and con sides of an argument, or they can be more subtle, such as two narrative fictions on similar themes. Every double passage will always be followed by at least some questions that ask to relate the two passages together. Students should expect this and look to understand the overlap between passages *as they first read them*.

What Doesn't Align

Note that the ACT aligns with all of these standards except the note about "two or more" themes. It's not clear why this was excluded—the test's survey does not give detailed explanations for why certain aspects do or do not align—but the most likely explanation is the length of the passages. Passages on the test are short—only one two-column page on average—so they generally won't have the kinds of multiple themes one might encounter in a longer text.

Summary

ACT questions frequently ask students to summarize or identify main themes of the passages. Additionally, finding the main ideas of a passage is a key strategy for all reading passages, to help with time management, comprehension of the passage, and answering the questions.

Sample ACT Questions

Main Idea Questions: 1.3.28, 1.3.34, 2.3.27, 3.3.31

3. Development and Interaction

Code	Standard	Aligns
R.CCR.3	**Analyze how and why individuals, events, and ideas develop and interact over the course of a text.**	**Y**
RL.11-12.3	Analyze the impact of the author's choices regarding how to develop and relate elements of a story or drama (e.g., where a story is set, how the action is ordered, how the characters are introduced and developed).	**P**
RI.11-12.3	Analyze a complex set of ideas or sequence of events and explain how specific individuals, ideas, or events interact and develop over the course of the text.	**Y**

Alignment

The ACT is aligned with the CCR Anchor and both grade-specific standards, excluding the word "drama" in the Literature standard.

Discussion

What Aligns

This standard is to some extent a continuation of standard 2. The development of a text is closely related to the progression of its central themes. As such, finding main ideas of each paragraph and the passage as a whole will help understand this development much the same way it helps understand the progression of themes. This can be on a literal level of the setting, events, or actions described, or on a more abstract level of the ways and reasons that ideas change over the course of the text.

This standard has an additional component of how "the author's choices" relate to the development of the text. This concept will be actively tested on the ACT. *Strategy Questions* are those that ask about the author's choices and tactics in the construction of the text. For example, these questions can ask about why the passage was ordered a certain way, how one section relates to the passage as a whole, or what rhetorical strategies the author employs. But Strategy Questions aren't the only type of questions that are relevant to this standard; Inferential Questions, Main Idea Questions, even Explicit Questions can deal with the development and interaction of ideas, too.

What Doesn't Align

The ACT does not align with the Literature standard's mention of "drama", since drama is excluded from the reading passages on the ACT. While some passages may talk about drama, all passages themselves will be in prose.

Summary
Finding the main ideas in a passage can help students identify how the events and ideas develop throughout the text. The ACT will ask questions about how and why an author makes particular choices in the structure and development of the text.

Sample ACT Questions
1.3.26, 2.3.21, 3.3.24

Craft and Structure

4. Meaning of Words

Code	Standard	Aligns
R.CCR.4	**Interpret words and phrases as they are used in a text, including determining technical, connotative, and figurative meanings, and analyze how specific word choices shape meaning or tone.**	**Y**
RL.11-12.4	Determine the meaning of words and phrases as they are used in the text, including figurative and connotative meanings; analyze the impact of specific word choices on meaning and tone, including words with multiple meanings or language that is particularly fresh, engaging, or beautiful. (Include Shakespeare as well as other authors.)	**P**
RI.11-12.4	Determine the meaning of words and phrases as they are used in a text, including figurative, connotative, and technical meanings; analyze how an author uses and refines the meaning of a key term or terms over the course of a text (e.g., how Madison defines faction in Federalist No. 10).	**Y**

Alignment

The ACT is aligned with the CCR Anchor and both grade-specific standards, excluding the phrase "or language that is particularly fresh, engaging, or beautiful. (Include Shakespeare as well as other authors.)" in the Literature standard.

Discussion

What Aligns

Determining the meanings of specific words in a text is an integral part of the ACT, most prominently seen in *Vocabulary-in-Context Questions*. These questions ask for the meaning of a specific word as it is used in a specific instance in the passage. For these questions, it is not enough for students to know the meaning of the word; they must also look at the context of the sentence. Vocabulary-in-Context Questions often use common words in uncommon senses. In fact, these questions usually have incorrect distractor choices that could be valid definitions of the word in other contexts.

While Vocabulary-in-Context Questions are common on the ACT, these questions are a subtype of a larger category called *Meaning Questions*. Meaning Questions do not necessarily ask for the meaning of individual words; questions also may ask for the meaning of a longer phrase, or even the meaning of a sentence in relation to the rest of the paragraph. But all share the same concept of using the context to detect subtleties in meaning.

The ACT also asks questions about tone. *Tone Questions* might ask for the tone of the entire passage or a single paragraph. Often these questions can simply be done by determining whether the tone is positive, negative, or neutral, but sometimes students will need to be more particular. On the ACT, Tone Questions are a subtype of a larger category called Generalization Questions, which might ask for other generalizations beyond the tone of the author's text, such as characterizations of people or events in the passage.

What Doesn't Align

The ACT excluded the phrase "language that is particularly fresh, engaging, or beautiful" from their alignment. While the ACT does ask about the color and tone of the language an author uses, the test does not ask students to make *value judgments* about the passage. Students do not have to like the passage; they just have to understand it. Questions about whether a passage is "beautiful", then, fall outside the scope of the test.

Since drama is outside the scope of the ACT, the test will not use selections from Shakespeare in a reading passage. Similarly, primary documents such as the Federalist Papers are unlikely to be used as reading passages on the test. However, these are just given as examples, and the principles and question types discussed here can be easily applied to any text.

Summary

The ACT will ask questions about the specific meaning of a word in a specific context in the passage. The test may also ask questions about the tone of sections of a passage.

Sample ACT Questions

Vocabulary-in-Context Questions: 2.3.15, 3.3.25, 3.3.39

Meaning Questions: 1.3.6, 1.3.33, 3.3.20

5. Structure of Texts

Code	Standard	Aligns
R.CCR.5	**Analyze the structure of texts, including how specific sentences, paragraphs, and larger portions of the text (e.g., a section, chapter, scene, or stanza) relate to each other and the whole.**	**Y**
RL.11-12.5	Analyze how an author's choices concerning how to structure specific parts of a text (e.g., the choice of where to begin or end a story, the choice to provide a comedic or tragic resolution) contribute to its overall structure and meaning as well as its aesthetic impact.	**Y**
RI.11-12.5	Analyze and evaluate the effectiveness of the structure an author uses in his or her exposition or argument, including whether the structure makes points clear, convincing, and engaging.	**P**

Alignment

The ACT is aligned with the CCR Anchor and both grade-specific standards, excluding the phrase "and evaluate the effectiveness of" in the Informational Text Standard.

Discussion

What Aligns

Structural questions such as these show up in the *Strategy Questions* mentioned for standard 3 above. Strategy Questions are those that ask about the author's choices and tactics in the construction of the text. For example, these questions can ask why the passage was ordered a certain way, how one section relates to the passage as a whole, or what rhetorical strategies the author employs.

Finding main ideas can also help identify quirks in the structure of the passage. Once students write down the main ideas for each paragraph, they will have a neat outline of the passage in the margins of the page. Examining the progression of ideas in that outline will help see how different sections of the passage relate to each other to form the larger narrative or argument. (It should also be mentioned that students don't have to strictly divide their main ideas by paragraphs. If, for example, one long paragraph contains two discrete ideas in it, it's perfectly fine to write two main ideas for the two sections of the paragraph.) Main

Idea Questions, which ask directly about the main ideas of the passage, often also relate these themes to the overall structure and development of the passage.

What Doesn't Align

The ACT does not align to the portion of the Informational Text standard referring to "effectiveness" for the same reason that it did not align to the mention of "beauty" in standard 4 above. The test does not ask students to make value judgments or decide whether the author's argument is persuasive. All they must do is determine what the author's argument says.

Summary

The ACT will ask questions about how and why an author makes particular choices in the structure and development of the text. Finding the main ideas in a passage can help students identify how the different sections of the text relate to each other and to the passage as a whole.

Sample ACT Questions

1.3.31, 2.3.13, 3.3.11

6. Point of View and Purpose

Code	Standard	Aligns
R.CCR.6	**Assess how point of view or purpose shapes the content and style of a text.**	**Y**
RL.11-12.6	Analyze a case in which grasping point of view requires distinguishing what is directly stated in a text from what is really meant (e.g., satire, sarcasm, irony, or understatement).	**Y**
RI.11-12.6	Determine an author's point of view or purpose in a text in which the rhetoric is particularly effective, analyzing how style and content contribute to the power, persuasiveness, or beauty of the text.	**N**

Alignment

The ACT is aligned with the CCR Anchor Standard and the Literature standard. The ACT is not aligned with the Informational Text standard.

Discussion

What Aligns

The point of view or purpose of a text is frequently an explicit topic of questions on the ACT. Questions that ask about the purpose of a text are usually categorized as Main Idea Questions since they deal with the overall themes and content of the passage. Indeed, writing main ideas can help students understand purpose and point of view better. Main ideas seek to distill the content of a paragraph to a single sentence or phrase. But this needn't just be the content of the paragraph; it can and should include elements of the purpose of a paragraph, such as whether the author is giving an objective description or making an argument. The purpose of a passage is often directly related to the type of text it is—narrative, informative, or persuasive—so it can be useful for students to be able to recognize these distinctions.

Even when not specifically addressed in the question, identifying the purpose or point of view of the passage can be key to comprehension. For example, questions that ask about the tone of the passage often hinge on the distinction between actively condemning an unpleasant event and objectively describing it.

We've also already seen how Strategy Questions can identify the choices that an author makes in constructing the text. One element of these choices is the decision to use certain rhetorical devices, such as irony or understatement. Such devices are explicitly tested on the ACT.

What Doesn't Align

The ACT does not align with this Informational Text Standard, likely for the same reasons we saw for standards 4 and 5. The test does not ask students to make a value judgment or decide whether the author's argument is effective, persuasive, or beautiful.

Summary

The point of view, purpose, and rhetorical devices employed in a passage are all material that is explicitly tested by the ACT.

Sample ACT Questions

Purpose: of a sentence: 3.3.2, 3.3.29; of a paragraph: 2.3.34; of the passage: 1.3.21, 2.3.31

Point of View: 1.3.1, 3.3.21

Integration of Knowledge and Ideas

7. Diverse Formats and Media

Code	Standard	Aligns
R.CCR.7	**Integrate and evaluate content presented in diverse formats and media, including visually and quantitatively, as well as in words.**	**PS**
RL.11-12.7	Analyze multiple interpretations of a story, drama, or poem (e.g., recorded or live production of a play or recorded novel or poetry), evaluating how each version interprets the source text. (Include at least one play by Shakespeare and one play by an American dramatist.)	**N**
RI.11-12.7	Integrate and evaluate multiple sources of information presented in different media or formats (e.g., visually, quantitatively) as well as in words in order to address a question or solve a problem.	**PS**

Alignment

None of these standards align with the ACT Reading Test. The CCR Anchor and the Informational Text standards do align with the ACT Science Test, with the exception of the words "and media". The Literature standard is not aligned with the ACT.

Discussion

What Aligns

This standard seems difficult to align, since the ACT reading is entirely text based. Obviously, there are no images or recordings on the test's reading sections. However, the ACT does align to this standard in the Science section.

The ACT Science is entirely about quantitatively evaluating content. Despite the name, it does not primarily test students on their knowledge of scientific facts. Rather, it is composed of six or seven passages, each of which comprises some combination of tables, graphs, figures, and explanatory texts. These figures present data in a wide variety of different formats: line graphs, shaded area graphs, scatterplots, diagrams, and all sorts of unusual combinations of axes. Some questions ask students to extract data from the tables and graphs. Others ask them to compare and combine data from multiple figures, or to combine data from the figures with information in the explanatory text.

In this way, the ACT Science Test is very similar to the ACT Reading Test. It does contain a great deal of science content, but everything the student needs to know and understand is defined and explained in the passage itself. The questions focus on the students' ability to find and evaluate information given in the text as well as in a variety of visual and quantitative figures.

What Doesn't Align

The ACT does not align with presentations in other "media". The test will only be offered on paper. There will be no digital, audio, or video components to the test.

The Literature standard does not align with the ACT partly because the test will not contain any poems or drama. However, this grade-specific standard is a fairly narrow application of the CCR Anchor Standard, and there are other ways to apply the Anchor to works of literature. Test material can be expanded beyond its intended scope to include this standard. For example, a class can take a passage from a practice test and conduct research to find other texts across different media that address the same topic in different ways. These texts can include print sources like periodicals, and web sources like blogs, news sites, videos, or podcasts. Alternatively, each test contains passages with topics in the Humanities, which often address specific writers, artists, or works. Students can select one of these passages and seek out the primary sources it describes, or look for other articles or texts with different interpretations of the works.

The point is that just because the tests themselves are stuck in print media does not mean that your class discussion has to be. Reading passages can be springboards into a wide array of topics for conversation, research, and analysis.

Summary

Alignment

The ACT includes questions with varied visual and quantitative formats on the Science section.

Beyond Alignment

Reading passages do not appear in varied media, but passages can be used for additional projects that delve into other media.

Sample ACT Questions

Any ACT Science Test will show a wide array of different figures and tables. For example, compare the following figures from test 1 in *The Official ACT Prep Guide*:

> Passage I, Figure 1: An anatomical diagram of a deer mouse's fur pigmentation along with four line graphs.
> Passage II, Figure 1: A drawing illustrating the set up of an experiment described.
> Passage IV, Figure 1: a bar graph with two axes.
> Passage V, Table 1: a table with six rows and four columns, including numbers and arrows showing directions.

8. Evaluate Arguments

Code	Standard	Aligns
R.CCR.8	**Delineate and evaluate the argument and specific claims in a text, including the validity of the reasoning as well as the relevance and sufficiency of the evidence.**	**YRS**
RL.11-12.8	(Not applicable to literature)	–
RI.11-12.8	Delineate and evaluate the reasoning in seminal U.S. texts, including the application of constitutional principles and use of legal reasoning (e.g., in U.S. Supreme Court majority opinions and dissents) and the premises, purposes, and arguments in works of public advocacy (e.g., The Federalist, presidential addresses).	**N**

Alignment

The ACT Reading and Science Tests are aligned with the CCR Anchor Standard. The ACT is not aligned with the Informational Text standard.

Discussion

What Aligns

Not all passages on the ACT are persuasive texts. However, those that are often have questions about the strength and logic of the argument. For example, a question may ask "which of the following, if true, would weaken the author's argument?" This does not require the student to actually take a position, but it does require the student to determine what facts would or would not affect the logical force of the argument.

These types of issues show up particularly frequently on ACT double passages. Often the two passages will present opposing sides of an issue. One passage will directly address the argument presented in the other, and questions ask students to identify how the authors respond to each other's' evidence.

Questions like this may also appear on the ACT Science Test. Reasoning Questions are those which ask whether the information in the tables and figures support a certain conclusion. These questions demand not only a yes or no answer, but ask students to supply appropriate evidence to support that conclusion. Additionally, Conflicting Viewpoints passages present a problem or situation followed by two or more hypotheses that attempt to explain it. The questions focus on the students' ability to follow the logic of an argument and contrast opposing points of view. For example, a question might present a new fact and ask which, if any, of the hypotheses is strengthened by this fact.

What Doesn't Align

The Informational Text standard does not align with either test. While passages on the tests may discuss American history and the foundation of the country, these primary texts themselves will not appear as passages.

Summary

The ACT asks questions evaluating the force and logic of an argument when persuasive texts appear as passages. The ACT Science may ask questions about conclusions that can be drawn from data, and in particular will evaluate the strength of arguments made in Conflicting Viewpoints passages. The ACT does not test seminal U.S. texts.

Sample ACT Questions

Conflicting Viewpoint Passages: 1.4.14–20, 2.4.28–34, 3.4.27–33

9. Multiple Texts

Code	Standard	Aligns
R.CCR.9	**Analyze how two or more texts address similar themes or topics in order to build knowledge or to compare the approaches the authors take.**	**YRS**

Code	Standard	Aligns
RL.11–12.9	Demonstrate knowledge of eighteenth-, nineteenth- and early-twentieth-century foundational works of American literature, including how two or more texts from the same period treat similar themes or topics.	N
RI.11–12.9	Analyze seventeenth-, eighteenth-, and nineteenth-century foundational U.S. documents of historical and literary significance (including The Declaration of Independence, the Preamble to the Constitution, the Bill of Rights, and Lincoln's Second Inaugural Address) for their themes, purposes, and rhetorical features.	N

Alignment

The ACT is aligned with the CCR for the Reading and Science Test. The grade-specific standards do not align with the ACT.

Discussion

What Aligns

The CCR Anchor Standard aligns very well with the ACT double passages, the point of which is to analyze how two texts address similar themes and to compare the authors' approaches.

Each ACT will have one double passage. Double passages will present two passages on similar or overlapping themes. Understanding the connection between the two authors' arguments or perspectives is often crucial to double passage questions. The relationship between the passages may be as simple as the pro and con sides of an argument, or they can be more subtle, such as two narrative fictions on similar themes. Every double passage will always be followed by at least some questions that ask to relate the two passages together. Students should expect this and look to understand the overlap between passages as they first read them.

As we've already seen, the ACT Science Test will contain one Conflicting Viewpoints passage. These passages are similar to double passages on the Reading Test in that they present multiple viewpoints describing the same issue or topic. Questions will often ask about the relationship between the viewpoints, where they agree and disagree, and the relative strengths of their arguments.

Because these passages appear on the Science Test, the questions will be concerned only with the content of the arguments, not the nature or quality of the author's writing. The questions often delve more deeply into the logic of the hypotheses argument. In contrast, the double passage on the Reading Test might also have questions regarding the differences in tone, form, or rhetorical strategies of the passages.

What Doesn't Align

As was mentioned previously, foundational texts of American history and literature do not appear on the ACT, so the two grade-specific standards do not align with test.

Summary

The ACT Reading Test contains one double passage with questions asking students to compare and contrast the texts. The ACT Science Test contains one Conflicting Viewpoints passage in which students must compare multiple hypotheses on a single topic. The ACT will not contain American foundational documents.

Sample ACT Questions

Double Passages: 1.3.18–20, 2.3.28–30

Range of Reading and Level of Text Complexity

10. Text Complexity

Code	Standard	Aligns
R.CCR.10	**Read and comprehend complex literary and informational texts independently and proficiently.**	**Y**
RL.11-12.10	By the end of grade 11, read and comprehend literature, including stories, dramas, and poems, in the grades 11–CCR text complexity band proficiently, with scaffolding as needed at the high end of the range. By the end of grade 12, read and comprehend literature, including stories, dramas, and poems, at the high end of the grades 11–CCR text complexity band independently and proficiently	**P**
RI.11-12.10	By the end of grade 11, read and comprehend literary nonfiction in the grades 11–CCR text complexity band proficiently, with scaffolding as needed at the high end of the range. By the end of grade 12, read and comprehend literary nonfiction at the high end of the grades 11–CCR text complexity band independently and proficiently.	**Y**

Alignment

The ACT is aligned with the CCR Anchor and Informational Text Standards. It is aligned with the Literature standard with the exception of the words "dramas, and poems".

Discussion

Text complexity was a major concern in the development and creation of the Common Core State Standards. Studies had found a wide gap between the complexity level of texts read in high school and those read in the first year of college—a gap that actually had been widening over time.

Of course, determining the appropriate complexity of a text can be difficult, but there are resources available to help. The Common Core website has some materials describing their methods for determining complexity, particularly Appendix A of the main ELA document on their website.

The ACT goes to great lengths in selecting the appropriate passages to use for their reading sections. While individual passages will vary in their complexity and difficulty, the overall reading level of the passages is appropriate for grades 11 to 12.

On the other hand, one of the great advantages of spending time preparing for the tests is that even students with poor reading skills can substantially improve their performance on difficult, complex texts. The nature of the test is such that students do not need to have a complete understanding of a passage to do well on the questions. Through a combination of finding main ideas, going back to the passage, anticipating, and eliminating, students can drastically cut down on the amount of work they need to put into a passage. Large chunks of a passage can be ignored because no questions ask about it. Difficult questions can be done easily because, while the correct answer involves subtle understanding of the passage, the wrong answers can be eliminated quickly.

It may seem that these kinds of techniques and preparation run counter to the spirit of the standards, that this is a way to use tricks to answer the questions without actually improving reading skills. But that is not the case at all. On the contrary, these techniques are simply the first step in showing students that complex passages that seem impenetrable are in fact perfectly comprehensible. Low-scoring students with poor reading skills are often frightened by the prospect of reading long passages. This fear can fester because students do not realize how much they already understand, how much they are already capable of doing. A-List's techniques directly work to counter this fear.

What does this mean for the classroom? The basics of the techniques' focus on reducing the amount of work students must do. If your only concern is test preparation, you can stop there. But if you want to continue to push students' reading skills, you can continue to discuss passages and questions long after all the answers have been found. Even though a paragraph is never mentioned in the questions, talk about how it relates to the rest of the passage. Even though you've eliminated all the wrong answers, keep discussing a question until students understand why the correct answer is correct. The techniques are a starting point, not an end point.

And of course, there is certainly no shortage of questions that require a nuanced understanding of a difficult passage. Students aiming for the highest scores on the test will have to read closely and carefully in order to get the most difficult questions. The tests are long enough that you can tailor the same material to the whole spectrum of ability. You can adjust your demands to match your students' skills to make sure that every student is pushed to the edge of his or her potential.

Summary

Alignment

ACT passages are chosen so as to be appropriately complex for grades 11–12. For struggling students, many test-taking techniques aim to simplify otherwise complex tests.

Beyond Alignment

For struggling students, the test is flexible enough that classroom activities can be adjusted to match the appropriate reading level for your students.

Writing

Overview

There are ten CCR Anchor Standards for Writing. These are organized into four groups of similar concepts. Each section below lists the Anchor Standard followed by the grade-specific standard for grades 11–12. For most of the standards, the grade-specific standards are broken down into a number of distinct but related skills.

Each standard in this section is aligned against the Writing Test (the test's essay) not the English Test (the multiple-choice questions) unless otherwise marked. The multiple-choice sections will be addressed in the Language strand.

The majority of the Writing standards are aligned with the ACT. If you spend time preparing for the test, you can be confident you are helping students acquire and refine real skills they will need and use in college or careers.

The ACT Writing Test is an optional section. If you are running a test prep course, you may find yourself spending less time on the essay and more time on the grammar multiple-choice questions. That's fine; those questions are important and also align with the Core Standards. But feel free to spend more time on writing essays if you want additional work on honing students' writing skills beyond what is necessary for the test. The prompts for the ACT essay are excellent exercises both inside and outside the confines of the test.

Here are some options for how to treat the test's essay:

- ◆ For test prep classes, you can assign them as the test intends under time constraints.
- ◆ For test prep classes, you can workshop topics, outlines, and practice essays in small or large groups.
- ◆ Outside test prep classes, you can give them as stand-alone homework assignments to practice writing on a small scale.
- ◆ Outside test prep classes, you can push them well beyond the intended short time and space constraints, into longer essays, multimedia presentations, or even research projects.

In general, because most of these standards apply to the essay prompts, the discussions here will not refer to sample questions. Each of the three tests in *The Official ACT Prep Guide* has an essay prompt at the end.

Text Types and Purposes

This section addresses the three main types of essays students should be able to write: persuasive, informative, and narrative. The three standards here apply similar skills to each of those three essay types.

In general, the *ACT aligns well with persuasive and informative essays, but not with narrative essays*. The prompt for the ACT essay asks students to discuss and evaluate three contrasting perspectives on a given topic. This fits well with standards asking students to write persuasive essays (the students will have their own thesis about the topic that must be defended) and informative essays (the students should accurately describe what the given perspectives say). However, it is not well suited for narrative essays: students should address the given essay, not write fiction or describe personal events.

Each of the Anchor Standards has subskills that are roughly parallel in what they address.

- ◆ 1a, 2a, and 3a address the establishment of the essay's topic.
- ◆ 1b, 2b, and 3b address the essay's development.
- ◆ 1c, 2c, 2d, and 3c address the language and sentence structure.
- ◆ 1d, 2e, and 3d address the style and tone.
- ◆ 1e, 2f, and 3e address the conclusion of the essay.

Most of these, in general, align to the ACT essay and are explicitly mentioned in the rubric for essay scoring. It should also be noted that many of these skills (particularly c, e, and f) are also explicitly tested in the multiple-choice English questions, which can contain persuasive, informative, and narrative passages.

1. Write Arguments

Code	Standard	ACT
W.CCR.1	**Write arguments to support claims in an analysis of substantive topics or texts, using valid reasoning and relevant and sufficient evidence.**	**P**
W.11-12.1a	Introduce precise, knowledgeable claim(s), establish the significance of the claim(s), distinguish the claim(s) from alternate or opposing claim(s), counterclaims, reasons, and evidence.	**Y**

(Continued)

Code	Standard	ACT
W.11-12.1b	Develop claim(s) and counterclaims fairly and thoroughly, supplying the most relevant evidence for each while pointing out the strengths and limitations of both in a manner that anticipates the audience's knowledge level, concerns, values, and possible biases.	Y
W.11-12.1c	Use words, phrases, and clauses as well as varied syntax to link the major sections of the text, create cohesion, and clarify the relationships between claim(s) and reasons, between reasons and evidence, and between claim(s) and counterclaims.	P
W.11-12.1d	Establish and maintain a formal style and objective tone while attending to the norms and conventions of the discipline in which they are writing.	N
W.11-12.1e	Provide a concluding statement or section that follows from and supports the argument presented.	P

Alignment

The ACT is aligned with the CCR Anchor with the exception of the phrases "or texts" and "and sufficient". The ACT is completely aligned with standards 1a and 1b. The ACT is aligned with 1c with the exception of the phrase "to link the major sections of the text". The ACT is not aligned with 1d. The ACT is aligned with 1e with the exception of the phrase "or section".

Discussion

What Aligns

The ACT essay is rigidly constructed to be a persuasive essay, almost like a debate topic. The prompt introduces an issue and briefly outlines its context. The prompt then includes three contrasting perspectives on the issue followed by the essay task to "write a unified, coherent essay in which you evaluate multiple perspectives on" the topic.

The student's argument must be supported by relevant reasoning and evidence beyond those given in the prompt. All three given perspectives must be mentioned and discussed. The student's language must be precise, varied, and generally error-free. All of these elements strongly align with the standards listed here.

What Doesn't Align

The ACT does not align with the phrase "or texts" in the CCR Anchor because the essay prompt is confined to a specific given topic. It's unclear why the ACT does not require that the evidence be "sufficient"; perhaps that phrase was excluded from alignment because the essay is intended to be a first draft, written in a short time period, so the evidence used is not expected to be exhaustive.

The ACT's qualification of standards 1c and 1e imply that the test does not require a student's essays to have distinct sections. Whether this aligns would depend upon your definition of "section", but again, the exclusion is presumably due to the abbreviated length of the assignment.

The ACT does not align with 1d. The essay is not confined to any particular discipline that might have its own norms or conventions. Additionally, the ACT's set of skill standards does not include any reference to maintaining a formal or objective tone. It does expect students to maintain a *consistent* tone, so that words and sentences don't stick out or seem incongruous with the rest of the passage. But it makes no requirements about formality or objectivity. (Indeed, having a bias might actually improve the force of an essay that strenuously argues one side.) It's curious that the alignment document does not consider this aligned to the *English* test, which does sometimes explicitly test errors of inconsistent tone.

Of course, just because the ACT does not make this demand of its students does not mean that you, the teacher, can't do so. When reviewing sample work essays, you can certainly call attention to instances in which student writing is noticeably informal or seems to demonstrate bias. Rather than simply banning such language, you can open up discussions of how and when such language would or would not be appropriate. You can include discussions of how the format or medium of the text can dictate the tone—for example, the difference between a newspaper article and an editorial, or between an article and a blog post.

Summary

Alignment

The ACT is favorable to writing persuasive essays and is structured for writing logical arguments. The essay requires a clear point of view, evidence or examples, and sophisticated, varied language.

Beyond Alignment

The ACT essay does not require a particular tone or style, but such questions are easily addressed in discussions of student writing.

2. Write Informative Texts

Code	Standard	Aligns
W.CCR.2	**Write informative/explanatory texts to examine and convey complex ideas and information clearly and accurately through the effective selection, organization, and analysis of content.**	**Y**
W.11-12.2a	Introduce a topic; organize complex ideas, concepts, and information so that each new element builds on that which preceded it to create a unified whole; include formatting (e.g., headings), graphics (e.g., figures, tables), and multimedia when useful to aiding comprehension.	**P**
W.11-12.2b	Develop the topic thoroughly by selecting the most significant and relevant facts, extended definitions, concrete details, quotations, or other information and examples appropriate to the audience's knowledge of the topic.	**Y**
W.11-12.2c	Use appropriate and varied transitions and syntax to link the major sections of the text, create cohesion, and clarify the relationships among complex ideas and concepts.	**Y**
W.11-12.2d	Use precise language, domain-specific vocabulary, and techniques such as metaphor, simile, and analogy to manage the complexity of the topic.	**Y**
W.11-12.2e	Establish and maintain a formal style and objective tone while attending to the norms and conventions of the discipline in which they are writing.	**N**
W.11-12.2f	Provide a concluding statement or section that follows from and supports the argument presented (e.g., articulating implications or the significance of the topic).	**P**

Alignment

The ACT is completely aligned with the CCR Anchor and standards 2b and 2d. The ACT is aligned with standard 2a with the exception of the final clause, "include formatting (e.g., headings), graphics (e.g., figures, tables), and multimedia when useful to aiding comprehension". The ACT is aligned with 2c with the exception of the phrase "to link the major sections of the text". The ACT is not aligned with 2e. The ACT is aligned with 2f with the exception of the phrase "or section".

Discussion

What Aligns

The ACT essay is necessarily a persuasive essay, but it is also well positioned for writing an informative essay, albeit not a purely informative essay. The two types share many characteristics, such that many of the standards listed above still align well with the ACT. The test requires students to develop and maintain a strong point of view. The essay's argument must be supported by relevant reasoning, examples, and evidence. The student's language must be precise and generally free of errors, and the sentence structure must be varied. All of these elements strongly align with the standards listed here.

What Doesn't Align

The most obvious departure from the limits of the ACT occurs in standard 2a. Because this is a hand-written test given over a short time period, the ACT does not allow any sort of formatting, graphics, or multimedia presentations. However, such elements can certainly be included if a topic from the test is used for longer assignments or research projects outside of test prep. For example, ACT essays could be bolstered with data in graphs or tables.

The previous discussion of style and tone discussed for standard 1d above applies equally to standard 2e here. The notes about "texts" and "sections" for standards 1c and 1e apply equally to standards 2c and 2f here. See standard 1 above for more details. Once again, several of these standards appear to align well to the multiple-choice English test, but the alignment document curiously made no mention of it.

Summary

Alignment

The ACT essay is necessarily persuasive but shares many characteristics with informative essays. The ACT's essays require a clear point of view, evidence or examples, and sophisticated, varied language.

Beyond Alignment

The ACT essay does not permit electronic formatting or visual aids, but such elements can be included if topics are used for longer projects outside of test prep. The essay does not require a particular tone or style, but such questions are easily addressed in discussions of student writing.

3. Write Narratives

Code	Standard	Aligns
W.CCR.3	**Write narratives to develop real or imagined experiences or events using effective technique, well-chosen details, and well-structured event sequences.**	**N**
W.11-12.3a	Engage and orient the reader by setting out a problem, situation, or observation and its significance, establishing one or multiple point(s) of view, and introducing a narrator and/or characters; create a smooth progression of experiences or events.	**N**
W.11-12.3b	Use narrative techniques, such as dialogue, pacing, description, reflection, and multiple plot lines, to develop experiences, events, and/or characters.	**N**
W.11-12.3c	Use a variety of techniques to sequence events so that they build on one another to create a coherent whole and build toward a particular tone and outcome (e.g., a sense of mystery, suspense, growth, or resolution).	**N**
W.11-12.3d	Use precise words and phrases, telling details, and sensory language to convey a vivid picture of the experiences, events, setting, and/or characters.	**N**
W.11-12.3e	Provide a conclusion that follows from and reflects on what is experienced, observed, or resolved over the course of the narrative.	**N**

Alignment

The ACT is not aligned with any of these standards.

Discussion

The ACT essay effectively does not permit narrative essays. While the test instructions don't explicitly require persuasive essays, the format makes it difficult to write anything else. The prompts are constructed in such a way that attempts at narration would not satisfy the demands of the test. It should be noted, however, that the English test does sometimes contain narrative passages, and students are expected to edit it with reference to tone, details, or appropriate conclusions.

Summary

The ACT essay does not permit narrative writing.

Production and Distribution of Writing

4. Clear and Coherent Writing

Code	Standard	Aligns
W.CCR.4	**Produce clear and coherent writing in which the development, organization, and style are appropriate to task, purpose, and audience.**	**P**
W.11-12.4	(Grade-specific expectations for writing types are defined in standards 1–3.)	–

Alignment

The ACT is aligned with this standard, with the exception of the phrases "and style" and "and audience".

Discussion

What Aligns

This standard is essentially a combination of the first three (as is evidenced by the note referring to grade-specific standards 1–3). The goal of any of these essays is to produce clear and coherent writing. As we saw in each of the first three standards, all of the grade-specific standards specifically address the development, organization, and style of the essays, as well as adhering to a clear and specific purpose.

What Doesn't Align

The ACT does not align with the mention of "style" for the same reason it does not align with standards of style addressed in standards 1, 2, and 3. The test requires a consistent style throughout the essay but does not demand any particular style.

Summary

The ACT essay requires students to produce clear and coherent writing. The ACT requires students to be attentive of their essays' development, organization, and purpose.

5. Revise and Strengthen Writing

Code	Standard	Aligns
W.CCR.5	**Develop and strengthen writing as needed by planning, revising, editing, rewriting, or trying a new approach.**	**PE**
W.11-12.5	Develop and strengthen writing as needed by planning, revising, editing, rewriting, or trying a new approach, focusing on addressing what is most significant for a specific purpose and audience. (Editing for conventions should demonstrate command of Language standards 1–3 up to and including grades 11–12.)	**PE**

Alignment

The ACT English Test is partially aligned with both the CCR Anchor and the grade-specific standard; for both standards, only the following words are highlighted "strengthen writing as needed by . . . revising, editing".

Discussion

What Aligns

It seems like these standards do not align well with the essays that we have been discussing. As we've said, the ACT's essay is intended to be a first draft written in a short period of time. Students need all the allotted time just to produce the draft; they hardly have any time to reread, revise, or rewrite the draft. However, while the essays cannot be revised during the test, the skills involved in revising and strengthening one's writing are very much apparent in the multiple-choice English section of the test.

These standards align well with the ACT English Test, which is set up to mimic the process of editing a finished draft, making necessary revisions for grammar, style, and coherence. The test is composed of five passages on a variety of topics. The questions attached to the passage take two basic forms: a word or phrase in the passage is underlined and students must choose the best word or phrase to go in that spot, attending to the grammar, style, and punctuation of the sentence; or, the question will ask whether a certain revision—such as moving, inserting, or deleting a phrase or sentence—should be made and why. Both of these formats represent the sort of questions students should ask themselves when reviewing their own writing.

The parenthetical note in the grade-specific standard refers to the "Progressive Skills" discussed in the Language strand.

What Doesn't Align

As we said, because of time limits, significant revision is not within the scope of the essays on the tests themselves. However, while you can't revise very much during the test, editing, revision, and discussion can be very prominent parts of your preparation for the test. This is a *second-level alignment*. Look at essays that students wrote under time constraints for practice tests and discuss what makes them strong and what needs improvement. Discuss ways of improving these essays with the class as a whole. The better students understand how to make their writing strong, the easier it will be for them to make it strong in the first place, during real test conditions.

Furthermore, you can expand your work on the essays beyond the scope of the tests. Use the prompts from the tests to make longer assignments. Have students workshop their essays together. Have them revise those essays in depth to make complete, refined second drafts. These activities clearly go beyond what the tests require of them, but can still be valuable tools to strengthen their writing skills.

Summary

Alignment
The ACT's essay has a time limit that is too short to permit serious revisions, but the multiple-choice English Test is designed to mimic the act of revising a piece of writing.

Beyond Alignment
The ACT's writing assignment can also be expanded to assignments that produce more polished drafts.

6. Use Technology

Code	Standard	Aligns
W.CCR.6	**Use technology, including the Internet, to produce and publish writing and to interact and collaborate with others.**	**N**
W.11-12.6	Use technology, including the Internet, to produce, publish and update individual or share writing products in response to ongoing feedback, including new arguments or information.	**N**

Alignment

The ACT is not aligned with either the CCR Anchor or the grade-specific standard.

Discussion

The ACT does not permit the use of any technology (with the exception of calculators, which are allowed only on the Math section of the test). Clearly, this standard is beyond the scope of basic preparation for the tests.

However, teachers can use test material to give assignments beyond the scope of the test in order to incorporate technology. We mentioned in the discussion of standard 5 above that teachers can continue essay writing assignments beyond the first draft to incorporate more editorial revision. Such assignments can also incorporate technology in different ways. For example, students can write their essays on computers and exchange drafts via email to critique each other's writing. Or students can create blogs in which they post drafts of their essays, and classmates can discuss them in the comments below. These projects can last a week or can continue throughout a semester.

Summary

The ACT does not permit the use of technology on its essay, but teachers can use the test's essay to come up with new assignments that use computer or Internet technology to revise and strengthen their writing.

Research to Build and Present Knowledge

7. Conduct Research

Code	Standard	Aligns
W.CCR.7	**Conduct short as well as more sustained research projects based on focused questions, demonstrating understanding of the subject under investigation.**	**N**
W.11-12.7	Conduct short as well as more sustained research projects to answer a question (including a self-generated question) or solve a problem, narrow or broaden the inquiry when appropriate; synthesize multiple sources on the subject, demonstrating understanding of the subject under investigation.	**N**

Alignment

The ACT is not aligned with either the CCR Anchor or the grade-specific standard.

Discussion

Like standard 6, this standard in itself does not align at all to the test, but it can align with additional tasks that push beyond the intended scope of the test.

The ACT's essay is intended to be a first draft written in a short period of time. Additionally, students will not have access to research material during the test. However, the prompts lend themselves quite well to expanded research projects.

For example, the prompt gives a general-interest contemporary topic with three perspectives on it. Students can research the issue of the topic and try to find real-world examples of the perspectives given. They can look for real evidence that support or refute these perspectives. They can find additional perspectives on the same issue. They can place the issue in a broader historical context. There are many possibilities for expanding the breadth of the task.

Summary

Extended research is beyond the scope of the ACT, but teachers can use the test's essay prompts as the basis for extended research projects.

8. Use Multiple Sources

Code	Standard	Aligns
W.CCR.8	**Gather relevant information from multiple print and digital sources, assess the credibility and accuracy of each source, and integrate the information while avoiding plagiarism.**	**N**
W.11-12.8	Gather relevant information from multiple authoritative print and digital sources, using advanced searches effectively; assess the strengths and limitations of each source in terms of the task, purpose, and audience; integrate the information into the text selectively to maintain the flow of ideas, avoiding plagiarism and overreliance on any one source and following a standard format for citation.	**N**

Alignment

The ACT is not aligned with either the CCR Anchor or the grade-specific standard.

Discussion

This standard is a natural extension of standard 7 discussed above. Like standard 7, this standard in itself does not align at all to the test, but it can align with additional tasks pushed beyond the intended scope of the test.

As discussed earlier, the ACT essay can be used as the basis of extended research projects. When assigning such projects, students can be required to use multiple print and digital sources. In so doing, they can analyze each source to assess its strengths and limitations and integrate the information into their own work. Their searches for this material lend themselves to classroom discussions about the reliability of information and how to assess a text's authority and accuracy.

Summary

Beyond Alignment

Extended research is beyond the scope of the ACT, but teachers can use the test's essay prompts as the basis for extended research projects. These research projects can draw on multiple print and digital sources and analyze their strengths and limitations.

9. Use Literary or Informational Texts

Code	Standard	Aligns
W.CCR.9	**Draw evidence from literary or informational texts to support analysis, reflection, and research.**	**N**
W.11-12.9a	Apply grades 11–12 Reading standards to literature (e.g., "Demonstrate knowledge of eighteenth-, nineteenth-, and early-twentieth-century foundational works of American literature, including how two or more texts from the same period treat similar themes or topics").	**N**
W.11-12.9b	Apply grades 11–12 Reading standards to literary nonfiction (e.g., "Delineate and evaluate the reasoning in seminal U.S. texts, including the application of constitutional principles and use of legal reasoning [e.g., in U.S. Supreme Court Case majority opinions and dissents] and the premises, purposes, and arguments in works of public advocacy [e.g., The Federalist, presidential addresses]").	**N**

Alignment

The ACT is not aligned with either the CCR Anchor or the grade-specific standards.

Discussion

These standards relate back both to the research discussed in standards 7 and 8 above and to the grade-specific standards discussed for the Reading strands. Standards 7 and 8 ask students to write research projects that include multiple outside sources. The CCR Anchor here asks students to include literature or literary nonfiction as sources. The grade-specific standards then demand that students treat those texts as we described in the strands for Reading Literature and Reading Informational Texts. (The examples quoted in the grade-specific standards above are RL.11-12.9 and RI.11-12.8 respectively, but all of the RL and RI grade-specific standards apply here.)

As stated before, actual research is outside the scope of the essays on the ACT, but teachers can adapt the prompts into longer research projects. These projects can use literary or informational texts as evidence and treat them appropriately within the students' work.

However, these standards actually can be relevant to the ACT if students so choose, depending on the particular essay prompt being addressed. While the ACT does not permit research during the test, it does expect students to supply evidence from their prior work in school, evidence that can be drawn from literary or informational texts. Students will not have direct access to any outside documents during the test, but they can and should be expected to be knowledgeable about whatever texts they choose to discuss. The test does not require students to use literature or literary nonfiction as evidence, but examples from American literature or American foundational documents are certainly within the scope of the essay. Any evidence is valid if it proves to be relevant to the given topic.

These texts can also be applied if the ACT prompt is used for research projects beyond the scope of the test. Through their research, students may find newspaper articles, case studies, or nonfiction texts that support their positions. Students should apply the Reading for Informational Texts standards when reading the texts and extracting evidence for their own writings.

Summary

The ACT does not support using these texts within the limits of the test, but such can be used in extended research projects beyond the scope of the ACT.

Range of Writing

10. Write Routinely

Code	Standard	Aligns
W.CCR.10	**Write routinely over extended time frames (time for research, reflection, and revision) and shorter time frames (a single sitting or a day or two) for a range of tasks, purposes, and audiences.**	**P**
W.11-12.10	Write routinely over extended time frames (time for research, reflection, and revision) and shorter time frames (a single sitting or a day or two) for a range of tasks, purposes, and audiences.	**P**

Alignment

The ACT is aligned with the following portion of the standard: "Write . . . over . . . shorter time frames (a single sitting) . . . for a range of tasks, purposes, and audiences." Note that the grade-level standard is identical to the CCR Anchor Standard.

Discussion

Obviously, the test's essay only permits writing over a short time frame. Writing routinely and writing over extended time frames do not fall within the scope of the tests.

However, one way to use test material to write routinely is to *do a lot of practice tests*. This is a second-level alignment. Probably the biggest difficulty in writing these essays is dealing with the time limit. If you are preparing your students for the ACT, they will need to practice writing these essays many, many times in the weeks before the test. Writing these essays routinely is highly recommended.

Furthermore, as we've already seen several times in the standards discussed above, the prompts can be applied to other projects beyond the constraints of the test itself. This is a third-level alignment. Think of the essay prompts for the ACT as raw materials that can be used on their own merits or as jumping off points for larger assignments. These assignments can be individual or group projects; they can be expositions or extensive research projects; they can be tightly timed or stretched over weeks. There are many ways the prompts can be used depending on what kind of skills you want to foster and strengthen in your students.

Summary

Beyond Alignment
Each individual essay is intended to take a short period of time, but students should practice by going through multiple prompts on a regular basis. Extended writing is beyond the scope of the ACT, but teachers can use the test's essay prompts as the basis for longer projects.

Language

Overview

The Language strand is the intersection of the Reading and Writing strands. Reading standards ensure students can comprehend entire texts; Writing standards ensure they can produce them. Language standards focus instead on the more elementary parts of texts—the words, the sentences, and the structures that lie beneath them.

There are six CCR Anchor Standards for Language. These are organized into three groups of similar concepts. Each section below lists the Anchor Standard followed by the grade-specific standard for grades 11–12. For most of the standards, the grade-specific standards are broken down into a number of distinct but related skills.

Additionally, the last section here will discuss the Progressive Skills standards. So far this document has focused on the grade-specific standards for grades 11–12, but remember that the Standards cover every year from kindergarten onwards. The grade-specific standards show what students in a particular grade should be learning with respect to the CCR, but they also presuppose that they've already learned a large swath of material earlier. When talking about something like the rules and conventions of grammar and usage, one often composes lists of the various rules that students need in order to be competent and fluent in the language. According to the standards' template, students will acquire those rules slowly over the course of their entire schooling. The Progressive Skills list outlines what these rules are and when students are expected to learn them.

(Of course, that doesn't mean your students actually will have done so. You may have to introduce them to concepts that, in the future when the standards are fully implemented, they should have learned in third grade.)

Because these language standards appear in several different areas of the tests, when a standard partially or fully aligns with the ACT, the tables below will list the letters of any and all subjects that the standard aligns with. The subjects are English (E), Math (M), Reading (R), Science (S), and Writing (W).

Technical note: For every standard in this strand, there is one main grade-specific standard for grades 11–12, which may then also have some subskills associated with it. Most of the time, the grade-specific standard is identical to the CCR Anchor, so we did not bother to list the main grade-specific standard, only the subskills. For example, L.CCR.1 is associated with L.11-12.1 (not shown), which is identical to L.CCR.1, but distinct from L.11-12.1a and L.11-12.1b. There is one exception to this template: L.11-12.4 below is similar but not exactly identical to L.CCR.4.

Conventions of Standard English

1. Grammar and Usage

Code	Standard	Aligns
L.CCR.1	**Demonstrate command of the conventions of standard English grammar and usage when writing or speaking.**	**PEW**
L.11-12.1a	Apply the understanding that usage is a matter of convention, can change over time, and is sometimes contested.	**PEW**
L.11-12.1b	Resolve issues of complex or contested usage, consulting references (e.g., *Merriam-Webster's Dictionary of English Usage*, *Garner's Modern American Usage*) as needed.	**N**

Alignment

The ACT English and Writing Tests are aligned with the CCR Anchor Standard with the exception of the phrase "or speaking". For grade-specific standard 1a, they are only aligned with the phrase: "Apply the understanding that usage is a matter of convention." The ACT is not aligned with standard 1b.

Discussion

What Aligns

The CCR Anchor is an excellent summary of the entire purpose of the ACT English and ACT Writing material. Effectively employing the rules and conventions of standard written English, whether that be in reviewing sentences and passages provided by the test or producing one's own writing, is obviously the central focus of all of these sections (though there is no speaking part on the ACT).

What Doesn't Align

The two grade-specific standards here, however, do not align well with the ACT. The test requires students to be familiar with the major rules of grammar and usage, but these standards go further to involve a kind of meta-commentary about what it means to be a rule of grammar and usage, how to determine whether something is a rule, and how these rules came to be. The ACT study is frankly being generous by awarding partial alignment to standard 1a; certainly the ACT requires students to follow the arbitrary conventions of English, but if a student does not understand the nature of that convention, he or she can still get the questions right.

The grade-specific standards seem oddly different from the CCR Anchor here. Why not discuss some of those specific rules of grammar and usage, rather than this meta-commentary? Remember, however, that the Standards are a set of standards for all grades starting in kindergarten. The standards listed for grades 11–12 are the last piece of the grammatical puzzle, the apotheosis of a lifetime of grammatical studies. Yes, the Standards expect students to be able to identify subject-verb agreement and shifts in verb tense, but they expect students to do so long before high school. See the "Progressive Skills" at the end of this chapter for a timeline of when students are expected to know various rules and conventions.

Issues regarding contested or evolving usage are outside the scope of the tests; in fact, the ACT generally does a good job of avoiding such issues so that every question will have unambiguously correct and incorrect choices. That said, there are certainly contentious constructions that appear on the test, issues that can be confusing and muddled even for experienced teachers, such as the appropriate use of passive or subjunctive verbs. Furthermore, some of the "rules" that are tested by the test are not universally accepted, such as the validity of singular "they". The works cited in the standard (particularly *Merriam-Webster's Dictionary of English Usage*) are excellent sources for further discussions of these topics. Additionally, there are several great websites and blogs, such as Language Log or John McIntyre's You Don't Say, that discuss some of these issues regularly and in depth.

While not required, discussions about these complex issues can be quite fruitful in class discussions about grammar. Such conversations can help instill a deeper understanding of linguistic principles in the students. Granted, if working with a class that struggles with grammatical issues, it's often best to avoid these more intricate discussions simply because the students need as much time as possible on the rules themselves. But to a certain extent, these conversations are unavoidable. Often students will ask "should I say *X* or *Y*", and the answer will be more complex than a simple binary answer. Being aware of the histories of these constructions can lead to deeper understanding.

Summary

Alignment
The ACT contains sections that are almost entirely devoted to assessing students' knowledge of the conventions of standard written English.

Beyond Alignment

The tests do not require students to have an understanding of complex, evolving, or contested usage, but conversations about them can be useful in instilling a deeper understanding of linguistic principles.

Sample ACT Questions

Any ACT English section will demonstrate alignment with the CCR Anchor Standard.

2. Orthography

Code	Standard	Aligns
L.CCR.2	**Demonstrate command of the conventions of standard English capitalization, punctuation, and spelling when writing.**	**PEW**
L.11-12.2a	Observe hyphenation conventions.	**N**
L.11-12.2b	Spell correctly.	**N**

Alignment

The ACT English and Writing Tests are aligned with the CCR Anchor Standard with the exception of the phrases "capitalization" and "and spelling". The ACT is not aligned with either grade-specific standard.

Discussion

The word "orthography" often refers solely to the spelling of words, but it can also have a broader sense referring to any set of characters and symbols used in writing, including capitalization, hyphenation, and punctuation. The ACT English test specifically and frequently tests punctuation. There will be about ten questions on each English test—13% of the test—that solely test knowledge of proper punctuation. The four choices for a given phrase will be worded the same, differing only in punctuation. Capitalization and hyphenation, in contrast, are not tested and will not be at issue on any questions. Spelling will not be tested with regard to words that are difficult to spell (like "accommodate" or "conscience"). However, students will be asked to choose between commonly confused words (like "their" vs. "they're" or "to" vs. "too"), which is at heart a spelling issue.

While the multiple-choice questions on the English test will not ask students about proper spelling, students will still be expected to use proper spelling in their essays, as the ACT Writing section requires students to adhere to "conventions of standard English grammar, usage, and mechanics". An essay with a few spelling mistakes can still score highly, but when those mistakes start to add up, it impedes the essay's readability and it can affect the score.

Summary

The ACT requires students to follow the rules of capitalization, spelling, punctuation, and hyphenation in their own writing. The ACT multiple-choice questions also raise issues of punctuation and spelling.

Sample ACT Questions

Punctuation: 1.1.3, 1.1.53, 2.1.33, 2.1.58, 3.1.20, 3.1.53

Spelling: 1.1.2, 1.1.50, 2.1.17, 3.1.14, 3.1.47

Knowledge of Language

3. Style and Meaning

Code	Standard	Aligns
L.CCR.3	**Apply knowledge of language to understand how language functions in different contexts, to make effective choices for meaning or style, and to comprehend more fully when reading or listening.**	**PERW**
L.11-12.3a	Vary syntax for effect, consulting references (e.g., Tufte's *Artful Sentences*) for guidance as needed; apply an understanding of syntax to the study of complex tasks when reading.	**PRW**

Alignment

The ACT English, Reading, and Writing Tests are aligned with the CCR Anchor Standard with the exception of the phrase "or listening". For the grade-specific standard, the ACT Reading and Writing tests are aligned only with the phrase "vary syntax for effect".

Discussion

Language standards 1 and 2 addressed the technical aspects of language: grammar, usage, punctuation, and other issues of mechanics. Standard 3 now introduces issues of *style*: not just using language correctly, but using language effectively. Using effective style is a major part of the ACT English section.

Questions on the ACT English section ask not only for the grammatically correct choice, but the most concise, most direct, or most precisely worded choice. Some questions will ask students not just to pick a grammatical phrasing, but an elegant phrasing—students must *improve* the sentence. Frequently questions will feature choices containing phrases that do not violate any rules of grammar or usage but are simply too long, too wordy, or too awkward. Furthermore, because the ACT English Test is made up of long passages, questions also may ask for the choice that most closely matches a style or tone already established in the passage.

Students not only need to be able to identify effective writing, they also need to be able to produce it themselves. The ACT's essay requires students to write clearly, effectively, and elegantly in order to communicate their point. Being free of errors of grammar and usage is only one element of effective use of language, and students must be able to use their knowledge of syntax and style toward strengthening their own writing.

Understanding the function of language is also relevant to the reading section. The ACT reading section often includes passages that contain tricky sections with complex sentence structures or common words applied to uncommon contexts. A deeper understanding of how these structures work and how meaning is shaped by context can be crucial to understanding what a passage is trying to say.

The grade-specific standard may seem a bit odd here, but remember that this is the grades 11–12 standard. Students will be expected to acquire more basic stylistic skills in earlier grades, as shown in the Progressive Skills table later in this section. The call to consult outside references is obviously beyond the scope of the test itself, as outside texts are not permitted. But an understanding of the effect of syntax is a fundamental concept of effective writing that will be relevant to understanding any text students read and producing coherent texts of their own.

Summary

The ACT requires students to be able to identify effective writing style on multiple-choice questions, produce effective writing in their essays, and understand complex structures in their readings.

ACT Sample Questions

Style Questions: 1.1.17, 1.1.58, 2.1.28, 2.1.57, 3.1.7, 3.1.43

Vocabulary Acquisition and Use

4. Determine the Meaning of Words

Code	Standard	Aligns
L.CCR.4	**Determine or clarify the meaning of unknown and multiple-meaning words and phrases by using context clues, analyzing meaningful word parts, and consulting general and specialized reference materials, as appropriate.**	**PR**
L.11-12.4	Determine or clarify the meaning of unknown and multiple-meaning words and phrases based on grades 11-12 reading and content, choosing flexibly from a range of strategies.	**PR**
L.11-12.4a	Use context (e.g., the overall meaning of a sentence, paragraph, or text; a word's position or function in a sentence) as a clue to the meaning of a word or phrase.	**YR**
L.11-12.4b	Identify and correctly use patterns of word changes that indicate different meanings or parts of speech (e.g., conceive, conception, conceivable).	**YE**
L.11-12.4c	Consult general and specialized reference materials (e.g., dictionaries, glossaries, thesauruses), both print and digital, to find the pronunciation of a word or determine or clarify its precise meaning, its part of speech, its etymology, or its standard usage.	**N**
L.11-12.4d	Verify the preliminary determination of the meaning of a word or phrase (e.g., by checking the inferred meaning in context or in a dictionary).	**N**

Alignment

The ACT Reading Test is aligned with the following portion of the CCR Anchor Standard and the identical L.11-12.4: "Determine or clarify the meaning of unknown and multiple-meaning words and phrases."

The ACT Reading test is fully aligned with standard 4a. The ACT English test is fully aligned with standard 4b. The ACT is not aligned with standards 4c and 4d.

Please note that the ACT alignment document does not specifically align 4a with Reading and 4b with English; rather, it lists all the grade-specific standards and their associated ACT English and Reading skills together. However, it is clear from the skills listed and the format of the test that this was the distinction the alignment intended.

Discussion

What Aligns

This standard is similar to R.CCR.4, "Interpret words and phrases as they are used in a text, including determining technical, connotative, and figurative meanings, and analyze how specific word choices shape meaning or tone." Whereas that standard referred to interpreting the subtle differences in word meanings, this standard specifically refers to words whose meanings are unknown or that have multiple potential meanings. These standards align well with the ACT.

The ACT does not have any heavily vocabulary-dependent questions, but determining the meanings of unknown words is still a part of the ACT Reading Test. Standard 4a closely describes the skill needed for Vocabulary-in-Context Questions. These questions ask for the meaning of a specific word as it is used in a specific instance in the passage. For these questions, it is not enough for students to know the meaning of the word; they must also look at the context of the sentence. Vocabulary-in-Context Questions may use unknown words or common words used with alternate, less common meanings. In fact, these questions usually have incorrect distractor choices that could be valid definitions of the word in other contexts. Standard 4d is relevant in this sense— students can guess the meaning of the word in isolation based on their existing knowledge of it, but must also verify its intended meaning in context.

Standard 4b aligns well with skills for the ACT English Test. Questions may ask students to select from multiple forms of a single word. These forms can test a number of different grammatical issues that require students to be able to distinguish parts of speech. For example, questions may present noun and verb forms of a given word within the same set of choices, or require students to change an adjective into an adverb. Other questions may require students to choose among different forms of a word within a given part of speech, such as the appropriate comparative or superlative form of an adjective.

What Doesn't Align

Standard 4c does not align well within the scope of the ACT since reference material is not permitted during the test. However, when reviewing practice material, we absolutely recommend students pick out all the words they did not know and physically look up their meanings in a dictionary to identify their meanings and alternate forms. In fact, A-List's suite of vocabulary materials includes several mechanisms that allow students to create their own lists of words: *The A-List Vocabulary Box* comes with blank flash cards, and *Vocab Videos* comes with an electronic flashcard generator, both of which can be used to add words to their existing vocabulary lists.

Summary
The ACT Reading Test asks questions about the specific meaning of a word in a specific context in the passage. The ACT English Test asks students to distinguish and choose between alternate forms of the same word.

Sample ACT Questions
Word Forms: 1.1.27, 1.1.41, 2.1.56, 3.1.38

5. Figurative Language and Nuance

Code	Standard	Aligns
L.CCR.5	**Demonstrate understanding of figurative language, word relationships, and nuances in word meanings.**	**YR**
L.11-12.5a	Interpret figures of speech (e.g., hyperbole, paradox) in context and analyze their role in the text.	**YR**
L.11-12.5b	Analyze nuances in the meaning of words with similar denotations.	**YR**

Alignment
The ACT Reading Test is aligned with the CCR Anchor and the grade-specific standards.

As is usually the case, there is a standard L.11-12.5 that is identical to the CCR Anchor Standard. For some reason, the ACT document deemed the CCR to be completely aligned, yet excluded the phrase "word relationships" from alignment with L.11-12.5. There is no indication for why this occurred, and by all measures word relationships are within the scope of the Reading Test. So we omitted L.11-12.5 and simply showed the CCR Anchor Standard here.

Discussion

As we've already seen, the ACT features Vocabulary-in-Context Questions that test students' understanding of the intended sense of a word as it's actually used in a passage. The choices for these questions are often similar enough to each other that they demand a subtle understanding of the word and the sentence.

In fact, attention to nuance is important throughout the reading section. Almost every question will contain choices that to the careless reader will sound similar to each other, and it requires a deeper understanding either of the passage or of the choices to be able to distinguish them properly.

Figures of speech are often present on reading passages of the ACT. As we saw in our discussion in the Reading strand, Strategy Questions are those which identify the choices that an author makes in constructing the text. One element of these choices is the decision to use certain rhetorical devices or figures of speech, such as irony, hyperbole, or paradox.

Summary

Alignment

Figurative language appears and is explicitly tested on the ACT Reading Test. Nuances of the meanings of words are important on the Vocabulary-in-Context Questions on the ACT Reading Test.

Sample ACT Questions

Figurative Language: 1.3.12, 1.3.32, 2.3.32

Vocabulary-in-Context Questions: 2.3.15, 3.3.25, 3.3.39

6. Learn More Words

Code	Standard	Aligns
L.CCR.6	**Acquire and use accurately a range of general academic and domain-specific words and phrases sufficient for reading, writing, speaking, and listening at the college and career readiness level; demonstrate independence in gathering vocabulary knowledge when considering a word or phrase important to comprehension or expression.**	**PERWS**
L.11-12.6	Acquire and use accurately a range of general academic and domain-specific words and phrases sufficient for reading, writing, speaking, and listening at the college and career readiness level; demonstrate independence in gathering vocabulary knowledge when considering a word or phrase important to comprehension or expression.	**PERWS**

Alignment

The CCR Anchor Standard is identical to the grade-specific standard. The ACT is aligned with the standard with the exception of the phrases "Acquire and" and "speaking and listening".

Discussion

Having a wide and diverse vocabulary is a crucial element to success on the Reading section of the ACT. On the Reading Test, vocabulary is explicitly important in some question types (such as Vocabulary-in-Context or Tone Questions), but the passages themselves, the questions about them, and the choices under the question all often contain difficult vocabulary.

The alignment notes for the ACT make a good point: From the test's perspective, the act of acquisition is irrelevant. The test only cares whether students know a word. It doesn't care how the students came to know it, whether through their own outside reading, through dedicated study of vocabulary words, or through cramming the night before the test.

However, this is a second-level alignment. For most kids, having a good vocabulary means acquiring more words. It is inevitable that there will be some words on the test that students won't know. A-List has several products to help acquire vocabulary. *The A-List Vocabulary Box* is a set of flashcards containing 500 words along with additional information about the words, such as synonyms, roots, and etymological notes. Additionally, A-List offers a web service called *Vocab Videos*, which contains short amusing videos that demonstrate the meanings of those 500 words. The videos form narrative episodes with recurring characters, and the website offers a wealth of additional tools for both students and teachers.

Of course, as we can see above, alignment with this standard goes well beyond the reading test. Vocabulary is a component to every section of the test:

♦ On the ACT English Test, students must understand how specific words relate to each other, such as the nuances in meaning that dictate the best word to choose for a sentence, or idiomatic rules dictating which preposition must follow a verb.
♦ On the ACT Essay, similar issues of word choice and vocabulary are very much in play. Proper and sophisticated use of language is one of the key areas upon which the essay will be judged.

- ◆ The ACT Science Test requires students both to know some key scientific terminology and to be able to figure out the meaning of other technical terms based on the information given in the passage.
- ◆ Even the Math section expects students to know the definitions of key mathematical terms such as "integer" or "slope". All subjects involve some reading, and all reading is inseparably linked to vocabulary.

Summary

Alignment

The ACT demands that students know and use vocabulary in a variety of subjects. Reading passages use sophisticated words, and questions ask about their nuances; multiple choice grammar questions ask about proper word choice, and the essay demands sophisticated vocabulary; ACT Science passages ask students to understand technical and scientific terminology.

Beyond Alignment

The test does not demand any particular method of vocabulary acquisition, but most students will invariably need to study vocabulary in some way.

Progressive Skills

Code	Skill	Aligns
L.3.1f	Ensure subject-verb and pronoun-antecedent agreement.	Y
L.3.3a	Choose words and phrases for effect.	Y
L.4.1f	Produce complete sentences, recognizing and correcting inappropriate fragments and run-ons.	Y
L.4.1g	Correctly use frequently confused words (e.g., to/too/two; there/their).	Y
L.4.3a	Choose words and phrases to convey ideas precisely. (Subsumed by L.7.3a)	–
L.4.3b	Choose punctuation for effect.	Y
L.5.1d	Recognize and correct inappropriate shifts in verb tense.	Y
L.5.2a	Use punctuation to separate items in a series (subsumed by L.9-10.1a).	Y

Code	Skill	Aligns
L.6.1c	Recognize and correct inappropriate shifts in pronoun number and person.	**Y**
L.6.1d	Recognize and correct vague pronouns (i.e., ones with unclear or ambiguous antecedents).	**Y**
L.6.1e	Recognize variations from standard English in their own and others' writing and speaking, and identify and use strategies to improve expression in conventional language.	**P**
L.6.2a	Use punctuation (commas, parentheses, dashes) to set off nonrestrictive/parenthetical elements.	**Y**
L.6.3a	Vary sentence patters for meaning, reader/listener interest, and style (subsumed by L.11-12.3a).	**Y**
L.6.3b	Maintain consistency in style and tone.	**Y**
L.7.1c	Place phrases and clauses within a sentence, recognizing and correcting misplaced and dangling modifiers.	**Y**
L.7.3a	Choose language that expresses ideas precisely and concisely, recognizing and eliminating wordiness and redundancy.	**Y**
L.8.1d	Recognize and correct inappropriate shifts in verb voice and mood.	**Y**
L.9-10.1a	Use parallel structure.	**Y**

Alignment

The ACT English Test is aligned with all Progressive Skills standards with the exception of skill L.6.1e, for which only the phrase "Recognize variations from standard English in their own and others' writing" is aligned. Standard L.4.3a was not included in the alignment document (presumably because it's subsumed by standard L.7.3a, which aligns the ACT.)

Discussion

What Aligns

The standards are made up of two components: the CCR Anchor Standards give the broad overall skills that students will ultimately need for success in college or a career, and the grade-specific standards that detail what aspect of those skills should be acquired by a given year. As we mentioned at the beginning of this chapter, this document focuses on the grade-specific standards for grades 11–12 since that's when students take the

ACT, but the standards cover every year from kindergarten onwards. The grade-specific standards show what students in a particular grade should be learning, but they also presuppose that they've already learned a large quantity of material earlier.

The table above outlines the component concepts and skills that students will need to acquire in order to meet CCR Anchor Standards by the end of high school.

The codes for each standard adhere to the same system the standards always use. The "L" means this is a standard in the Language strand. The first number shows the grade by which the standard should be met. The standards listed here start in grade 3 and run up to grades 9–10. The second number shows the CCR Anchor Standard to which the specific standard corresponds. All standards here correspond to Language standards 1, 2, or 3.

Note that the letters that follow the standard number are unique to that grade level's standards. Standard L.5.2a ("Use punctuation to separate items in a series.") is the first subpoint for the fifth grade under Language CCR Anchor 2; it is connected to L.CCR.2 ("Demonstrate command of the conventions of standard English capitalization, punctuation, and spelling when writing."), but has no particular relationship to skill 2a for other grades (such as L.11-12.2a, "Observe hyphenation conventions.")

These skills go as far back as third grade, but that doesn't mean they aren't relevant for 11th and 12th graders. The key word here is *progressive*; students should acquire each new skill in the order listed above, but they should also retain all the knowledge and skills acquired in previous years, so that they can build up to more and more complex ideas. This is why the 11–12 grade-specific skill for standard 1 discussed above involved the meta-commentary about complex and contested usage—such discussions are only possible after having spent a great deal of time reviewing all the nuts and bolts of the grammar.

As for the content of these progressive skills, they couldn't be better suited for the ACT. Every skill listed here will in some form be a part of the test. If one were to devise a list of rules that are tested on the multiple-choice sections of the ACT English, this would be a perfect template. Subject-verb agreement, pronoun-antecedent agreement, fragments, run-ons, tense, parallelism—it's as if the CCSSI created the Standards directly out of A-List's *Book of Knowledge*.

Once a reliable method for measuring degrees of longitude [1] <u>were discovered</u>, cartographers were able to draw accurate maps of the oceans.	**1.** A) NO CHANGE B) discovers C) was discovered D) would have discovered
Douglas hates using his debit card, believing that someone could easily steal it and gain access to his [2] <u>account, he prefers</u> using cash whenever he can.	**2.** A) NO CHANGE B) account. He prefers C) account he prefers D) account. Preferring

Question 1 has choices dealing with subject-verb agreement, tense, and voice. Question 2 has choices dealing with run-ons, fragments, and punctuation. Between two questions, we have addressed five standards.

What Doesn't Align
Only one item here does not perfectly align: Standard L.6.1e only partially aligns with the ACT, excluding the reference to speaking (obviously) and the phrase "identify and use strategies to improve expression in conventional language." But even if the multiple-choice questions do not assess this standard, it can be applied to students' own writing on the essays.

Summary
The Progressive Skills table is a veritable checklist of the grammatical rules and skills that are tested on the ACT. Virtually every one is prominent on the multiple-choice questions or specifically assessed on the essay.

Sample ACT Questions
Verb Agreement: 1.1.14, 2.1.11, 3.1.24

Pronoun Agreement: 1.1.42, 2.1.32, 3.1.33

Word Choice: 2.1.57, 2.1.66, 3.1.43

Fragment: 1.1.8, 2.1.49, 3.1.4

Run-on: 1.1.39, 2.1.61, 3.1.41

Verb Tense: 1.1.33, 2.1.53, 3.1.8

Comma use: 1.1.5, 1.1.21, 2.1.19, 2.1.47, 3.1.10, 3.1.50

Redundancy: 1.1.38, 1.1.46, 2.1.12, 2.1.30, 3.1.3, 3.1.26

Special Topics

Overview

Reading, Writing, and Language are the three main strands of the English Language Arts Standards, but there are a few other strands that we have not yet discussed. They were excluded from our earlier discussion because they have more narrow focus such that these strands are best discussed in isolation.

Some of these align poorly and some were excluded from the study altogether. But the ACT does still align with some of the standards here. As we've seen many times, even standards that are beyond the intended scope of the tests can be met by stretching and adapting test material.

In this section, we will address the following strands:

- Two content areas in the Reading strand: *Reading for Literacy in History/Social Studies (RH)* and *Reading for Literacy in Science and Technical Subjects (RST)*. Each has ten grade-specific standards that correspond to the ten CCR Anchor Standards for Reading.
- One content area in the Writing strand: *Writing Standards for Literacy in History/Social Studies, Science and Technology (WHST)*. These ten grade-specific standards correspond to the ten CCR Anchor Standards for Reading.
- An additional strand, *Speaking and Listening (SL)*. The tables show six new CCR Anchor Standards and six associated grade-specific standards.

The ACT includes all the strands in its study. The Speaking and Listening standards do not align with the ACT at all. Other strands align to varying degrees.

Reading for Literacy in History/Social Studies

Code	Standard	Aligns
Key Ideas and Details		
RH.11-12.1	Cite specific textual evidence to support analysis of primary and secondary sources, connecting insights gained from specific details to an understanding of the text as a whole.	**N**
RH.11-12.2	Determine the central ideas or information of a primary or secondary source; provide an accurate summary that makes clear the relationship among the key details and ideas.	**PR**
RH.11-12.3	Evaluate various explanations for actions or events and determine which explanation best accords with textual evidence, acknowledging where the text leaves matters uncertain.	**N**
Craft and Structure		
RH.11-12.4	Determine the meaning of words and phrases as they are used in a text, including analyzing how an author uses and refines the meaning of a key term over the course of a text (e.g., how Madison defines faction in Federalist No. 10).	**YR**
RH.11-12.5	Analyze in detail how a complex primary source is structured, including how key sentences, paragraphs, and larger portions of the text contribute to the whole.	**N**
RH.11-12.6	Evaluate authors' differing points of view on the same historical event or issue by assessing the authors' claims, reasoning, and evidence.	**N**
Integration of Knowledge and Ideas		
RH.11-12.7	Integrate and evaluate multiple sources of information presented in diverse formats and media (e.g., visually, quantitatively, as well as in words) in order to address a question or solve a problem.	**N**
RH.11-12.8	Evaluate an author's premises, claims, and evidence by corroborating or challenging them with other information.	**N**
RH.11-12.9	Integrate information from diverse sources, both primary and secondary, into a coherent understanding of an idea or event, noting discrepancies among sources.	**N**
Range of Reading and Level of Text Complexity		
RH.11-12.10	By the end of grade 12, read and comprehend history/social studies texts in the grades 11-CCR text complexity band independently and proficiently.	**YR**

Alignment

The ACT Reading Test is fully aligned with grade-specific standards 4 and 10. It is aligned with standard 2 with the exception of the phrase "primary or secondary". The ACT is not aligned with any of the other standards shown here.

Discussion

Each ACT Reading Test will have one Social Studies passage that discusses historical topics. Several of these standards, therefore, do align well with those passages. In fact, many of these grade-specific standards are similar or identical to the corresponding standards in the Reading for Informational Text standards discussed earlier. The ACT also contains double passages in which two authors present different perspectives on a common topic.

Standards 2, 4, and 10 here align well for the same reasons that the earlier RI standards did. Similarly, standard 1 does not align for the same reason RI.11-12.1 did not. See the main Reading section above for more details about how those standards align with the ACT.

Many of the History standards fail because ACT passages will generally be secondary sources, not primary sources. This explains why standards 3 and 5–9 all do not align. (In fact, standards 7–9 are very similar to the corresponding RI standards, which also did not align. RI.11-12.7 did align with the ACT Science Test, which is not relevant to topics in history.)

Summary

The ACT contains passages on historical topics. Some of these standards align in the same way the standards for Reading Informational Text do. Others do not align because the passages will be drawn from secondary sources. The ACT does contain double passages that present multiple perspectives on a topic.

Reading for Literacy in Science and Technical Subjects

Code	Standard	Aligns
Key Ideas and Details		
RST.11-12.1	Cite specific textual evidence to support analysis of science and technical texts, attending to important distinctions the author makes and to any gaps or inconsistencies in the account.	**PR**
RST.11-12.2	Determine the central ideas or conclusions of a text; summarize complex concepts, processes or information presented in a text by paraphrasing them in simpler but still accurate terms.	**YR**
RST.11-12.3	Follow precisely a complex multistep procedure when carrying out experiments, taking measurements, or performing technical tasks; analyze the specific results based on explanations in the text.	**YS**
Craft and Structure		
RST.11-12.4	Determine the meaning of symbols, key terms, and other domain-specific words and phrases as they are used in a specific scientific or technical context relevant to grades 11–12 texts and topics.	**PR**
RST.11-12.5	Analyze how the text structures information or ideas into categories or hierarchies, demonstrating understanding of the information or ideas.	**YR**
RST.11-12.6	Analyze the author's purpose in providing an explanation, describing a procedure, or discussing an experiment in a text, identifying important issues that remain unresolved.	**YR**
Integration of Knowledge and Ideas		
RST.11-12.7	Integrate and evaluate multiple sources of information presented in diverse formats and media (e.g., quantitative data, video, multimedia) in order to address a question or solve a problem.	**PS**
RST.11-12.8	Evaluate the hypotheses, data, analysis, and conclusions in a science or technical text, verifying the data when possible and corroborating or challenging conclusions with other sources of information.	**YS**
RST.11-12.9	Synthesize information from a range of sources (e.g. texts, experiments, simulations) into a coherent understanding of a process, phenomenon, or concept, resolving conflicting information when possible.	**YS**
Range of Reading and Level of Text Complexity		
RST.11-12.10	By the end of grade 12, read and comprehend science/ technical texts in the grades 11-CCR text complexity band independently and proficiently.	**YRS**

Alignment

The ACT Reading Test is aligned with standards 1, 2, 4, 5, 6, and 10, with the exception of the word "technical" in standards 1 and 4. The ACT Science Test is aligned with standards 3, 7, 8, 9, and 10, with the exception of the phrases "and media" and "video, multimedia" in standard 7.

Discussion

Like the Reading for Literacy in History/Social Studies standards, these standards take the Reading CCR Anchor Standards and apply them to a specialized content area, in this case, science. And like those standards, these align well with the relevant passage on the ACT Reading Test. Each Reading Test will contain one passage on Natural Science, to which some of these standards align well for the same reasons the corresponding Informational Text and History/Social Science standards did. Others don't align for the same reason the corresponding standards don't: chiefly, because the passages are not primary texts. See those two strands for more details about this alignment.

However, the ACT also contains a Science Test, which addresses this shortcoming of the Reading Test. The Science Test contains six to seven passages that do present original material. Each passage contains a textual introduction which is accompanied by a variety of tables and graphs—information presented in multiple formats (standard 7)—that the students must analyze and evaluate directly on their own merits (standard 8). Research Summaries passages present detailed multistep procedures (standard 3), and students must answer questions about their design and results. Furthermore, the Conflicting Viewpoints passage is specifically designed to present two or more differing hypotheses on a given topic or situation, followed by questions asking students to compare the arguments and attempt to resolve discrepancies (standards 7, 8, and 9).

For further discussion of the Science Test, see our book, *ACT Math in the Classroom*.

Summary

Between the Science Test and the science passage on the Reading Test, the ACT is aligned with all of these standards. The Reading Test will ask questions about how the central ideas and construction of the text itself. The Science Test will ask about the data, experiments, and conclusions contained in a text.

Writing for Literacy in History/Social Studies, Science, and Technical Subjects

Code	Standard	Aligns
WHST.11-12.1	Write arguments focused on discipline-specific content.	**N**
WHST.11-12.1a	Introduce precise, knowledgeable claim(s), establish the significance of the claim(s), distinguish the claim(s) from alternate or opposing claim(s), and create an organization that logically sequences the claim(s), counterclaims, reasons and evidence.	**N**
WHST.11-12.1b	Develop claim(s) and counterclaims fairly and thoroughly, supplying the most relevant data and evidence for each while pointing out the strengths and limitations of both claim(s) and counterclaims in a discipline-appropriate form that anticipates the audience's knowledge level, concerns, values, and possible biases.	**N**
WHST.11-12.1c	Use words, phrases, and clauses as well as varied syntax to link the major sections of the text, create cohesion, and clarify the relationships between claim(s) and reasons, between reasons and evidence, and between claim(s) and counterclaims.	**N**
WHST.11-12.1d	Establish and maintain a formal style and objective tone while attending to the norms and conventions of the discipline in which they are writing.	**N**
WHST.11-12.1e	Provide a concluding statement or section that follows from and supports the argument presented.	**N**
WHST.11-12.2	Write informative/explanatory texts including the narration of historical events, scientific procedures/experiments, or technical processes.	**N**
WHST.11-12.2a	Introduce a topic and organize complex ideas, concepts, and information so that each new element builds on that which preceded it to create a unified whole; include formatting (e.g., headings), graphics (e.g., figures, tables), and multimedia when useful to aiding comprehension.	**N**
WHST.11-12.2b	Develop the topic thoroughly by selecting the most significant and relevant facts, extended definitions, concrete details, quotations, or other information and examples appropriate to the audience's knowledge of the topic.	**N**
WHST.11-12.2c	Use appropriate and varied transitions and sentence structures to link the major sections of the text, create cohesion, and clarify the relationships among complex ideas and concepts.	**N**

(Continued)

Code	Standard	Aligns
WHST.11-12.2d	Use precise language, domain-specific vocabulary, and techniques such as metaphor, simile, and analogy to manage the complexity of the topic; convey a knowledgeable stance in a style that responds to the discipline and context as well as to the expertise of likely readers.	N
WHST.11-12.2e	Provide a concluding statement or section that follows from and supports the information or explanation provided (e.g., articulating implications or the significance of the topic).	N
WHST.11-12.3	(Not applicable as a separate requirement)	–
WHST.11-12.4	Produce clear and coherent writing in which the development, organization, and style are appropriate to task, purpose, and audience.	N
WHST.11-12.5	Develop and strengthen writing as needed by planning, revising, editing, rewriting, or trying a new approach, focusing on addressing what is most significant for a specific purpose and audience.	PE
WHST.11-12.6	Use technology, including the Internet, to produce, publish, and update individual or share writing products in response to ongoing feedback, including new arguments or information.	N
WHST.11-12.7	Conduct short as well as more sustained research projects to answer a question (including a self-generated question) or solve a problem; narrow or broaden the inquiry when appropriate; synthesize multiple sources on the subject, demonstrating understanding of the subject under investigation.	N
WHST.11-12.8	Gather relevant information from multiple authoritative print and digital sources, using advanced searches effectively; assess the strengths and limitations of each source in terms of the specific task, purpose, and audience; integrate information into the text selectively to maintain the flow of ideas, avoiding plagiarism and overreliance on any one source and following a standard format for citation.	N
WHST.11-12.9	Draw evidence from informational texts to support analysis, reflection, and research.	N
WHST.11-12.10	Write routinely over extended time frames (time for reflection, and revision) and shorter time frames (a single sitting or a day or two) for a range of discipline-specific tasks, purposes, and audiences.	N

Alignment

The ACT English Test is aligned with the phrase "strengthen writing as needed by . . . revising, editing" in standard 5. It is not aligned with any other standard.

Discussion

These standards do not align well with the ACT within their intended scope. The essays are not designed for discipline-specific writing.

Some of these Writing standards, like standards 1 and 2, correspond to CCR Anchors that align with the ACT, but these grade-specific standards require writing about particular "historical events, scientific procedures/ experiments, or technical processes" that don't align with the ACT essay prompt. (It may seem like, for example, standards 1a through 1e here align well with the ACT, but those are subskills under WHST.11-12.1, which requires "discipline-specific content".) Others, like standards 6 through 9, don't align because the Writing CCR Anchor didn't align in the first place. The only standard that does align here does so with the ACT English Test, not the Writing Test, just as W.CCR.5 did. See the discussion in the main Writing section above for more details.

The ACT essay is particularly ill-suited to discipline-specific writing like this because the topic is so specific to an issue relevant to the lives of high school students. But we've already seen how these essay prompts can be expanded to longer writing projects, projects that could certainly have a focus on either historical or scientific topics. For such projects, the level of detail the students go into with regard to technical subjects is entirely up to you the teacher, and if you are not prepared for or interested in going into heavy historical or scientific material with the students, then such writing projects would be better left to classes in those subject areas.

Summary

Beyond Alignment
The ACT Writing Test does not align well with these standards because the prompt is too narrow to support detailed historical and scientific content.

Speaking and Listening

Code	Speaking and Listening Anchor Standards	Aligns
Comprehension and Collaboration		
SL.CCR.1	Prepare for and participate effectively in a range of conversations and collaborations with diverse partners, building on others' ideas and expressing their own clearly and persuasively.	–
SL.CCR.2	Integrate and evaluate information presented in diverse media and formats, including visually, quantitatively, and orally.	–
SL.CCR.3	Evaluate a speaker's point of view, reasoning, and use of evidence and rhetoric.	–
Presentation of Knowledge and Ideas		
SL.CCR.4	Present information, findings, and supporting evidence such that listeners can follow the line of reasoning and the organization, development, and style are appropriate to task, purpose, and audience.	–
SL.CCR.5	Make strategic use of digital media and visual displays of data to express information and enhance understanding of presentations.	–
SL.CCR.6	Adapt speech to a variety of contexts and communicative tasks, demonstrating command of formal English when indicated or appropriate.	–

Code	Speaking and Listening Standards for Grades 11–12 (SL)	Aligns
Comprehension and Collaboration		
SL.11-12.1	Initiate and participate effectively in a range of collaborative discussions (one-on-one, in groups, and teacher-led) with diverse partners on grades 11–12 topics, texts, and issues, building on others' ideas and expressing their own clearly and persuasively.	–
SL.11-12.1a	Come to discussions prepared, having read and researched material under study; explicitly draw on that preparation by referring to evidence from texts and other research on the topic or issue to stimulate a thoughtful, well-reasoned exchange of ideas.	–
SL.11-12.1b	Work with peers to promote civil, democratic discussions and decision-making, set clear goals and deadlines, and establish individual roles as needed.	–

Code	Speaking and Listening Standards for Grades 11–12 (SL)	Aligns
SL.11-12.1c	Propel conversations by posing and responding to questions that probe reasoning and evidence; ensure a hearing for a full range of positions on a topic or issue; clarify, verify, or challenge ideas and conclusions; and promote divergent and creative perspectives.	–
SL.11-12.1d	Respond thoughtfully to diverse perspectives; synthesize comments, claims, and evidence made on all sides of an issue; resolve contradictions when possible; and determine what additional information or research is required to deepen the investigation or complete the task.	–
SL.11-12.2	Integrate multiple sources of information presented in diverse formats and media (e.g., visually, quantitatively, orally) in order to make informed decisions and solve problems, evaluating the credibility and accuracy of each source and noting any discrepancies among the data.	–
SL.11-12.3	Evaluate a speaker's point of view, reasoning, and use of evidence and rhetoric, assessing the stance, premises, links among ideas, word choice, points of emphasis, and tone used.	–
Presentation of Knowledge and Ideas		
SL.11-12.4	Present information, findings, and supporting evidence, conveying a clear and distinct perspective, such that listeners can follow the line of reasoning, alternative or opposing perspectives are addressed, and the organization, development, substance, and style are appropriate to purpose, audience, and a range of formal and informal tasks.	–
SL.11-12.5	Make strategic use of digital media (e.g., textual, graphical, audio, visual, and interactive elements) in presentations to enhance understanding of findings, reasoning, and evidence to add interest.	–
SL.11-12.6	Adapt speech to a variety of contexts and tasks, demonstrating command of formal English when indicated or appropriate. (See grades 11–12 Language standards 1 and 3 for specific expectations.)	–

Alignment

This strand was not included within the scope of the ACT alignment study.

Discussion

Obviously, the ACT does not contain any speaking or listening elements, so none of these standards align to the test. However, while they do not align with skills students use during the test, they align well with skills they use during preparation for the test. This is a second-level alignment. Speaking and listening are obviously large components of all classroom activities. Almost any element of either test can be adapted into classroom activities that involve students giving presentations to the class, evaluating other students' presentations, or working together in groups.

The activities described here are particularly well suited to normal preparation for the ACT's essay. They perfectly describe the kinds of conversations that occur during the normal process of workshopping these essays, either in small groups or as a whole class. Students can discuss potential examples to support their theses, discuss how different perspectives interact with each other, or write full paragraphs and present them to their peers for feedback. All of these activities can help students develop critical thinking skills and rhetorical skills that can carry over to their writing, as well.

The references to alternate media in standards 2 and 5 go beyond normal preparation for the essay. But as discussed earlier, teachers who are interested in focusing on these skills can use test material for extended projects that incorporate digital media or visual presentations.

Speaking and listening activities also need not be limited to essay material. The number of potential group activities teachers can conceive of is limitless. Students can give group presentations analyzing or assessing reading passages. They can take sides in reading double passages or Science Conflicting Viewpoints passages. They can create projects around vocabulary work, either academic, like researching common etymologies, or creative, like writing skits or narratives using key words. Virtually anything you assign students to do in class can be adapted to align with these standards.

Summary

Beyond Alignment

There is no speaking or listening component on the ACT. However, these activities are a normal part of classroom activities when preparing for the ACT's essay. Furthermore, teachers can create and assign collaborative activities centered on almost any element of the test.

3

Reading Assignments

Probably the most crucial element of preparation for the Reading section of the ACT is *practice*. The point of the Reading section is to test whether students can understand a text, and students who are not strong readers cannot improve without spending time actually *reading*. But there's no reason you have to limit yourself to ACT material—there are things to read all around us. Even a passage as short as a single paragraph has a main idea, explicit statements, and implicit conclusions. You can take almost any passage at all, have students read it, and ask them questions about what they've read.

This document will help guide you through this process. We will give you tips on how to find an appropriate passage and how to write questions for it that reflect the kinds of questions that ACT Reading questions ask. The nice thing about the test is that there's little variation in the format and question types. Once you become familiar with it, it's easy to adapt existing texts into ACT-style passages.

While this document specifically discusses ACT preparation, drills like this can be used for other purposes too. You can use these drills for SAT preparation as well, since SAT Reading questions are mostly identical to ACT questions. Or you can use them as pure reading comprehension drills for your regular English classes. The goal here is simply to get students to read effectively and efficiently.

Choosing a Passage

Here are some tips for choosing a text to use for your reading drill.

1. Passages should be around 750 words.

ACT passages are around 700–800 words, so that's a good length to aim for. Most newspaper articles tend to run slightly longer than that, but still well within reason. You should avoid anything over 1,000 words. Not only is it more difficult to keep students' attention that long, but longer articles will often present more complicated arguments or situations and provide more information than is necessary for our purposes. Of course, if you see a long article on a topic you like, you can always just use a smaller portion of it.

But remember too this is your class, not the real ACT. The degree to which you adhere to the 700- to 800-word limit is determined by the degree to which you want your drill to mimic a real ACT passage. If you want to make your assignment just a short quiz, great: use a one-paragraph passage with two questions. If you want it to be a larger project, you can pick something like a long-form article. Just know that the farther you stray from 800 words, the less your passage will resemble the real ACT.

2. Use online newspapers.

Online newspapers are perhaps the best and easiest source of freely available passages. They have articles on a variety of topics, usually written in clear but sophisticated language. Opinion pieces and editorials can be good sources because they're short and they have points of view and arguments, as opposed to more objective journalistic articles. But regular informative articles can also be effective.

We often use *The New York Times* website, since it is one of the most popular and respected sites, and it has a good breadth of topics. But any newspaper, national or local, will do fine. Magazines like *The Atlantic* or Internet-only news sites like *Slate* can also provide good content. Popular science sites like *Discover Magazine* are good places to find science articles that don't require too much existing knowledge.

You can even use sources that are less high-brow. Websites about sports, fashion, television, or even personal blogs, can be used for these passages. In fact, using alternative material like this can show students that we read the same way no matter what we're reading. (If you do use non-newspaper Internet sources, you will want to be sure to read the articles carefully first. The Internet can get a little vulgar at times.)

Please note that some websites may require a paid subscription for full access to articles. Before asking students to read online articles on their own, make sure they'll all have free access to the content.

And of course, you needn't use the Internet; print newspapers and magazines work just as well, if you don't mind the extra photocopying.

Fiction passages also show up on the ACT, but it can sometimes be harder to create fiction passages yourself. Any piece of fiction will have to be excerpted—even short stories are generally too long for the test. You'd have to make sure that the excerpt you choose can stand alone without knowledge of the rest of the story, and that it doesn't require too much esoteric interpretation to understand. On the ACT, fiction passages sometimes begin with a one- or two-sentence introductory paragraph that sets the basic scene, but too much background will distract from our goal.

You can use books you're reading in your class anyway, of course. If you're talking about *The Great Gatsby*, why not write some ACT-style questions about it? Just be careful to keep your questions limited to a specific passage without asking too much about larger themes that require understanding of the book as a whole. Remember that this is a test of reading comprehension, not a literature test.

3. Don't require outside knowledge.

Don't pick articles on topics that require too much outside knowledge. ACT passages are tests of how well students read, not how much they know. You don't want to penalize students who don't know much about the stock market, neurology, or international politics.

This doesn't mean you have to avoid complicated topics altogether. Science articles, for example, are often great sources of texts, because they're usually good about giving all the necessary background information in the articles themselves (and they often come with figures). The articles will address deep concepts, but you won't have to know anything ahead of time. This is why national newspapers are good sources for passages; they are written for a general audience and often don't assume much knowledge on the part of the reader. Conversely, more specialized sites will often assume that the reader knows more about the subject. Articles about baseball statistics, for example, will be over the heads of any students who don't know anything about baseball.

4. Avoid contentious topics.

Students may have strong opinions about certain political or religious topics like immigration, war, or abortion. Don't use articles that will start arguments among your students (or between you and your students). The point of these assignments is not to come to a resolution on a topic or to *find the Truth*; it's just to understand *what the author says*. All that matters is what the article says, *not* whether it's true.

(Of course, if your class is actually working on debate or on writing persuasive essays, you may want to discuss your students' own beliefs more. Do so at your own risk. But if you're only working on ACT prep, the students' own opinions on the topic are irrelevant to this assignment.)

5. Try a double passage.

Every ACT has one double passage, in which students are given two different passages on similar or overlapping topics. You can easily make your own double passages by finding two articles on the same topic or event. If you do so, make sure the articles are sufficiently different from each other. Don't pick two straight journalistic articles from two different papers, since they'll most likely be very similar in tone and content. Instead, pick two articles of different types, such as an objective reportage article and an opinion piece on the same event.

Note that the 700- to 800-word count applies to the whole pair of passages, so each should be around 350–400 words. If you choose two 800-word passages, that will end up being a bit long.

6. Beware of line numbering.

If you're working on ACT preparation, you will want your questions to occasionally have specific references to which part of the passage they're asking about. ACT passages come with line numbers, and many questions will give specific line numbers to let students know where in the passage they can find the answer. Obviously, most newspaper articles will not come with line numbers, so you will have to come up with a way to include these references.

If you're actually printing copies of the article, you can always write in line numbers by hand directly onto the paper. You don't have to number every line; ACT passages number every fifth line. Just make sure the line numbers you give in your questions properly match up to the passage.

If students are working on computers directly off of the Internet, be careful. Different browsers can use different font sizes or column widths, so line numbers may differ, too. A word that appears in line 10 on your screen may appear in line 14 on a student's screen. In this case, rather than using line numbers when giving references, you can count sentences and paragraphs, for example, "in the second sentence of paragraph two".

Keep in mind, however, that about 60% of the questions on the ACT Reading Test do not provide line references. This varies by question type; virtually all Meaning Questions have line references, whereas only about 20% of Explicit Questions do. Being able to locate evidence in the passage without line references is an important skill for students to practice.

Writing the Questions

After you choose an article, you need to come up with some questions about it. Real ACT Reading questions are all multiple choice, but you can leave your questions open-ended if you prefer. Writing effective answer choices is actually trickier and more time-consuming than it may seem. But the same skills and concepts are involved with open-ended questions, such as understanding main ideas, or going back to the passage to find evidence.

Students' answers to open-ended questions may vary wildly. As a result, some teachers might prefer to use these questions for group discussions instead of individual drills or homework, but that's up to you. If you are grading their responses, give students a little leeway if their responses aren't exactly what you expected, as long as they don't give too much, too little, or incorrect information.

Below we discuss the main question types of ACT Reading passage questions along with instructions for how to write your own. Sometimes we will provide a general question that can be asked about literally any passage. Other times we give a general template to be adapted to your passage or advice on how to craft specific questions about specific content.

How many questions should you write for each passage? As many as you like! The ACT asks ten questions per passage, but you don't have to stick to ten. A six-question drill with about one question per type is a pretty manageable length. You can also choose to focus on one particular question type if you want to practice a particular skill, for example, making just six Main Idea Questions. You probably don't want to include too many more than ten questions; anything longer than that will likely be too much for your students. But there's no limit to the number of questions you could potentially ask about a text, depending on the length of the passage, its content, and your own interest in the topic.

1. Explicit Questions

These are questions that ask about things the author explicitly states in the passage. They're fairly easy to write. The key is to make the questions very literal: *What does the passage say about [X]?* Ask about facts and stated opinions explicitly presented in the passage.

Here are some hypothetical examples to give you a sense of what these questions sound like:

- *In the second sentence of paragraph 3, "decreasing test scores" are given as an example of what?*
- *According to the passage, how are "the larger monkeys" (line 24) different from "standard monkeys" (line 18)?*
- *In paragraph 4, the author states that "this proposed law" will have what consequence?*

Note that all these questions give specific references to what part of the passage you're asking about, be it a line number or a description of the sentence and paragraph. The ACT sometimes gives specific line references, and learning to go back and check the passage is an important skill. Keep in mind that you don't have to point to the exact place where the answer is found; the answer to ACT questions are often found a sentence or two before or after the given line reference. But on the real test, Explicit Questions often don't have line references; the hard part of the question is figuring out where to find the answer.

Remember that we only care about what the passage *says*, not whether it's *true* in real life. Some of your students may have other ideas about what the consequences of "this proposed law" will be. That doesn't matter. We are just trying to understand what the passage says.

It's perfectly fine to have your students directly quote the passage in order to answer the question. This helps reinforce the idea that the answers to the questions are all grounded in direct evidence from the passage. However, you may also want to practice *translation*. On the ACT, the correct answer choice won't always use the exact same phrasing as the relevant line in the passage. Instead, the choice will have the same *meaning*, but use different words. It can be tough for some students to realize that a choice means the same thing as the line in the passage when it's worded differently. You may want to force your students to put their answers in their own words rather than quoting the passage to work on this skill. Doing so can also ensure that your students actually do understand the meaning of the passage, and they're not just blindly parroting the line.

2. Inferential Questions

Writing Inferential Questions can be tricky. An Inferential Question asks students to find information that is unstated but necessarily implied by the passage. There are two important words in that description: "unstated" and "necessarily".

First, make sure the answer isn't literally stated in the passage. Inferential Questions on the ACT often ask what the passage "suggests" or "implies" in a given line. But it's not enough to just use the word "suggest" in your question. You need to make sure that the answer isn't stated outright. (And that it isn't stated in different words elsewhere in the passage.)

Second, make sure that the implication you seek is *necessarily* implied by the passage. This is not an exercise in conjecture or prediction. It is very important that you prevent your students from jumping to conclusions about the author's beliefs. Many wrong answer choices on the ACT use exactly that kind of guesswork.

When writing Inferential Questions, you should go easy on your students. Making inferences is an abstract reasoning skill. It's one of the hardest things that students will have to do on the test. But these questions are a bit easier on the real ACT because students have four answer choices to scrutinize. They can pick up on clues given in the choices and eliminate those that are clearly false. Moreover, there may be multiple inferences that can be drawn from the line, and it may not be immediately obvious which one the question is asking for. If your questions don't have answer choices, you want to be sure to phrase them in such a way that helps students figure out specifically which inference you're looking for.

3. Meaning Questions

Meaning Questions ask how a particular word or phrase is being used in the passage. Not its purpose or tone, but what the phrase literally means or refers to.

◆ *In line [X], when the author says "[Y]", what does he mean by [Y]?*

In principle, these are just explicit questions that are phrased more explicitly. They virtually always have line references, so you know where to go. You simply have to translate the author's phrase into a different wording. Find the choice that means the same thing as they author's phrase.

Often, these take the form of Vocabulary-in-Context Questions. These question test two things: vocabulary and context. They always take the same form:

◆ *In line [X], the word "[Y]" most closely means what?*

It will be up to you to choose a word to ask about. When choosing, consider both the word itself and the context around it.

Newspaper articles can often use vocabulary that is unfamiliar to students, so you can include questions as a straight vocabulary test: *Do you know what this word means?* In fact, if you are giving a regular vocabulary assignment to your students, you can look for words from that assignment which appear in the passage.

While questions like that can be helpful for vocabulary building, Vocabulary-in-Context Questions on the ACT are usually a little trickier than that. They don't just test hard or unfamiliar words; in fact, often the word *isn't* unfamiliar. Rather, it will be a familiar word that has multiple meanings, and students must use the context of the sentence in which it appears to determine which meaning is intended. For example:

◆ *In line [X], the word "fast" most closely means what?*

Everyone knows "fast" means "at a high speed". It's so obvious, it's hard for kids to define it without using the word ("It's when you go, uh, fast. You know, fast.") But that's not the only definition of "fast". It can also mean "firm" or "tight" as in *fast friends* or *the rope was tied fast to the pier*. Or it can mean "deeply" as in *fast asleep*. Or it can be a verb meaning "to abstain from eating for a period of time". Students may know all of these meanings, but they will have to look at the context to determine which meaning is intended in this particular sentence in the passage.

You can also pick words whose meanings are hard but can be deduced based on the content of the sentences in which they appear. But you should avoid using words that are overly specialized for the topic of passage. Scientific words fall into this category, but all fields use specialized words, including politics, business, and even sports. Be careful not to ask questions that demand too much out-side knowledge. Our goal now is to help them learn to read effec-tively, not to teach them about mortgage insurance or electoral procedures.

On the real test, often these questions will have choices that are similar in meaning but have important nuanced differences. So you don't want to be too lenient in allowing vague student answers. It can be hard for students to define a word without being given choices, so some lengthy or periphrastic answers are fine, as long as they're as specific as can be. Go farther than just "good" or "bad".

4. Main Idea Questions

This is one of the most important question types and also one of the easiest to write. For every passage you use, you should ask:

◆ *What is the main idea of this passage?*

The answer to this question should *not* be a paragraph-long essay discussing the details of the author's argument. It should be a quick, one-sentence response briefly summarizing the article. All we're asking here is, *what is it about?* For an informative piece, it's a quick description of the events or content. For an editorial, it's a quick sum-mary of the position the author takes. For fiction, it's a summary of the action. It is not about nuance. You're basically asking to write a headline for the article.

You can also ask this question for individual paragraphs, for example:

◆ *What is the main idea of the first paragraph?*
◆ *What is the main idea of the second paragraph?*

For these questions, students should focus on the *content* and *argu-ment* of the paragraph in question, not necessarily mentioning its relationship to the article as a whole.

5. Generalization Questions

Generalization Questions ask students to make a short generaliza-tion about a large amount of information in the passage. They are similar to Main Idea Questions in that they ask about large sec-tions of the passage. But they don't necessarily point to specific paragraphs or sections of the passage. Rather, they're about themes and ideas that run throughout. Therefore, the answer to these questions may not be in a single place, so the questions rarely give line references. Generalization Questions may also ask about the tone, opinions, beliefs, or attitudes of any character in the passage.

◆ *It can reasonably be inferred from the passage as a whole that the narrator views her mother as:*

This question seems to take the form of an inferential question. The key difference is that it's not asking for an inference from a particular part of the passage, but from the passage as a whole. Students will have to look at the narrator's interactions with her mother throughout the entire passage and make a general characterization.

Tone Questions are a subset of Generalization Questions. These are relatively rare but easy to write. For any passage you use, you can ask:

◆ *What is the author's tone throughout the passage?*

Tone often comes down to positive/neutral/negative. The author argues for something, argues against something, or objectively reports facts. But of course, you can get more subtle and varied in your description of the author's tone.

For example, the author could be

- ◆ Angry
- ◆ Enthusiastic
- ◆ Sarcastic
- ◆ Alarmed
- ◆ Nostalgic

As you make more drills, try to pick articles with varied tones. Don't use ten articles that all have objective journalistic tone. Tones will more likely be varied in opinion and editorial pieces.

Remember also that the *tone* of a piece is not the same thing as the *content* of the piece. The author can be making a heavily biased argument on one side of an issue, yet still maintain an objective journalistic tone in his or her prose.

6. Strategy Questions

Strategy Questions ask about how the article is constructed and why the author made the choices that he or she did. These can be on a larger level about the structure of the article, or on a small level asking about specific rhetorical techniques.

On the larger structural level, you can ask about the relationship between individual paragraphs and the whole passage. For example:

◆ *What is the relationship between the first paragraph and the passage as a whole?*

For a straightforward piece of reportage, the first paragraph will often give a brief summary of the events or situations which the article will go on to describe (i.e., the main idea of the passage). Opinion articles may use the first paragraph to state the argument they will give. But some passages might use the first paragraph to give necessary background information, to provide an anecdote that will illustrate a larger point later, to present a point of view it will then argue against, or even tell a story that is only tangentially related to the overall point.

Of course, you don't have to ask about the first paragraph. You can ask about any paragraph in the essay that has an interesting or unexpected relationship to the passage as a whole. The last paragraph also often has an interesting relationship to the passage as a whole.

On the smaller rhetorical level, you can look at specific choices that the author makes in the article you chose. The key is to ask *why* the author does something, or what the *function* of a particular line is. Some hypothetical examples and some potential responses:

◆ *In paragraph X, why does the author quote this person?*
  - to give evidence for his or her position
  - to provide a counterargument to a previous point
  - to lighten the tone of the passage
◆ *The question in line Y serves what function?*
  - to ask a rhetorical question for which the answer is obvious
  - to present the issue that will subsequently be debated
  - to present a mystery whose answer is still unknown

Notice that the example responses to the example questions do not have to make specific reference to the *content* of the article; rather they describe the *structure* and *form* of the article.

7. Double Passage Questions

As we mentioned earlier, the ACT will contain a double passage. Double passages will present two passages on similar or overlapping topics. Many questions about double passages will be no different than regular questions, asking about particular details from one passage or the other. But some questions will ask students to identify or describe the relationship between the passages.

Finding two articles on the same topic is fairly easy to do. You could find two editorials that take opposite sides of an issue. You could find one objective report and one editorial. You could find two objective reports that are on different topics that have overlapping themes.

Double Passage Questions directly compare the form, content, or tone of the two passages. These can be questions of any type (explicit, inferential, strategy, etc.) as long as they address both passages. For example:

- *How would the author of Passage A most likely explain the "controversial results" mentioned in line 56 of Passage B?*
- *How would the author of Passage B most likely respond to the argument presented in paragraph 2 of Passage A?*
- *What person mentioned in Passage B holds views that are most similar to those of the author of Passage A?*
- *In comparison with Passage B, the tone of Passage A is more what?*
- *What rhetorical technique does Passage A employ that Passage B does not?*

Notice that these questions often ask for hypothetical responses: How *would* the author of Passage A respond to Passage B? But these questions are always grounded in the explicit statements made in the passage. Be careful not to read too much into it and delve into conjecture. For example, just because an author makes an argument from a conservative point of view on one issue does not necessarily mean he or she would agree with Republican platforms on other issues. Only rely on what's stated in the passages, not your own beliefs or outside knowledge.

Giving the Assignment

You can make these passages a regular assignment throughout the year, say once a week or every other week. Find a passage, write some questions, and give it to your students. Since all Reading passages take basically the same format, you don't have to worry too much about varying your format. You'll want to pick a range of different source passages, of course, both from your own class readings or outside sources.

You might not include all question types on every assessment, but make sure they all get covered over the course of the semester. It's okay if one particular quiz doesn't have a strategy question, but you'll want to get one in there at some point. To help you determine the priority of question types, the following table shows the approximate distribution of question types on the ACT:

Explicit questions	40%
Meaning questions	10%
Main idea questions	10%
Inferential questions	18%
Generalization questions	10%
Strategy questions	5%
Double passage questions	7%

Additional Assignments
Here are some ideas for other ways you can adapt this assignment:

1. Demand evidence for every question.
Because the ACT often does not include line references, you can require students to give line-reference information for *every* question. No matter the question type, don't give line references. Force the students to provide a specific sentence, or even a single word, that justifies their answer.

2. Write distractor choices.
As we've mentioned, one of the difficulties in multiple-choice tests like the ACT is the presence of distractor choices. These choices often aren't random—they're *tempting*. There are specific reasons why a student might believe that they're right.

It takes a long time to write choices for a question, so we wouldn't advise writing your own choices for all the questions. However, it's useful to provide students with at least one answer choice *that you explicitly tell them is wrong*. You can then ask the students, *why is this choice wrong*? What *specifically* makes it wrong? Give *specific textual evidence* proving that it's wrong.

This is exactly how the students should be approaching answer choices on the real test. There are three times as many wrong choices as there are right choices, so it's often easier to look for a wrong choice than it is to find the right choice. They should be going through the choices like a lawyer shooting down arguments, crossing out individual words that disqualify the entire choice.

3. Have students make the drills.

We've just talked about how easy it is to find passages and write questions—so why not have the kids do it themselves? Besides being less work for all of us (whoo!), getting them to see the principles behind the construction of the test can help them better understand what the test is asking them to do.

This can be a fun group project as well, with each member of a team doing a different step:

- Have Student A find a passage, either from texts you're already using in class or through their own research. If you like you can let them have fun with this and choose less serious texts to use as passages.
- Have Student B write questions about the passage. Make sure they're already familiar with the different question types before asking them to do this.
- Have Student C take the assignment and write full explanations for why the answers are correct.
- Have Student D write distractor choices and explain why they're wrong.

Or make an assembly line where each student does each step and then passes it to the right for the next step. At the end, you'll have four drills each of which was built by all four students. You can then even have that group swap drills with a different group and try each other's drills.

Sample Passage

The following passage was taken from the opening paragraphs of *Jude the Obscure* (1895), by Thomas Hardy.

[1] The schoolmaster was leaving the village, and everybody seemed sorry. The miller at Cresscombe lent him the small white tilted cart and horse to carry his goods to the city of his destination, about twenty miles off, such a vehicle proving of quite sufficient size for the departing teacher's effects. For the schoolhouse had been partly furnished by the managers, and the only cumbersome article possessed by the master, in addition to the packing-case of books, was a cottage piano that he had bought at an auction during the year in which he thought of learning instrumental music. But the enthusiasm having waned he had never acquired any skill in playing, and the purchased article had been a perpetual trouble to him ever since in moving house.

[2] The rector had gone away for the day, being a man who disliked the sight of changes. He did not mean to return till the evening, when the new school-teacher would have arrived and settled in, and everything would be smooth again.

[3] The blacksmith, the farm bailiff, and the schoolmaster himself were standing in perplexed attitudes in the parlour before the instrument. The master had remarked that even if he got it into the cart he should not know what to do with it on his arrival at Christminster, the city he was bound for, since he was only going into temporary lodgings just at first.

[4] A little boy of eleven, who had been thoughtfully assisting in the packing, joined the group of men, and as they rubbed their chins he spoke up, blushing at the sound of his own voice: "Aunt has got a great fuel-house, and it could be put there, perhaps, till you've found a place to settle in, sir."

[5] "A proper good notion," said the blacksmith.

[6] It was decided that a deputation should wait on the boy's aunt—an old maiden resident—and ask her if she would house the piano till Mr. Phillotson should send for it. The smith and the bailiff started to see about the practicability of the suggested shelter, and the boy and the schoolmaster were left standing alone.

[7] "Sorry I am going, Jude?" asked the latter kindly.

[8] Tears rose into the boy's eyes, for he was not among the regular day scholars, who came unromantically close to the schoolmaster's life, but one who had attended the night school only during the present teacher's term of office. The regular scholars, if the truth must be told, stood at the present moment afar off, like certain historic disciples, indisposed to any enthusiastic volunteering of aid.

[9] The boy awkwardly opened the book he held in his hand, which Mr. Phillotson had bestowed on him as a parting gift, and admitted that he was sorry.

[10] "So am I," said Mr. Phillotson.

[11] "Why do you go, sir?" asked the boy.

[12] "Ah—that would be a long story. You wouldn't understand my reasons, Jude. You will, perhaps, when you are older."

[13] "I think I should now, sir."

[14] "Well—don't speak of this everywhere. You know what a university is, and a university degree? It is the necessary hallmark of a man who wants to do anything in teaching. My scheme, or dream, is to be a university graduate, and then to be ordained. By going to live at Christminster, or near it, I shall be at headquarters, so to speak, and if my scheme is practicable at all, I consider that being on the spot will afford me a better chance of carrying it out than I should have elsewhere."

[15] The smith and his companion returned. Old Miss Fawley's fuel-house was dry, and eminently practicable; and she seemed willing to give the instrument standing-room there. It was accordingly left in the school till the evening, when more hands would be available for removing it; and the schoolmaster gave a final glance round.

[16] The boy Jude assisted in loading some small articles, and at nine o'clock Mr. Phillotson mounted beside his box of books and other *impedimenta*, and bade his friends good-bye.

[17] "I shan't forget you, Jude," he said, smiling, as the cart moved off. "Be a good boy, remember; and be kind to animals and birds, and read all you can. And if ever you come to Christminster remember you hunt me out for old acquaintance' sake."

Sample Questions

Main Idea Question

1. What happens in the passage?

Meaning Questions

2. As it is used in paragraph 1, sentence 2, what does *effects* mean?
3. As it is used in paragraph 14, sentence 5, what does *afford* mean?

Explicit Questions

4. According to the passage, why does Mr. Phillotson not take his piano with him?
5. According to the passage, why is Mr. Phillotson moving away?
6. How is Jude's reaction to Mr. Phillotson's departure different from that of the other students?

Inferential Question

7. Paragraph 2 suggests what about how the rector feels about Mr. Philloston's departure?

Generalization Question

8. Jude responds to Mr. Phillotson's departure with what emotion?

Answers and Explanations

The Passage

This passage is not a perfect example of a reading passage—not much happens here, it rambles at the end—so it's unlikely it would appear in this form on a real ACT. But we're not looking for a perfect reading passage. We're not actually writing an ACT; we're showing you can apply ACT skills to *any* passage. This passage is certainly satisfactory for our purposes: it's 717 words, right in our target range; it's the opening of the book, so it's fairly self-contained and doesn't require expository background; it has some difficult language, but not so much as to make the entire piece is incomprehensible. It's a good start for us.

Don't worry about explaining too much. You don't have to tell kids anything about the book, about what it's about, what happens later, the historical context. You might want to (it's really good!), but you don't have to. Just focus on what's written. You might also be tempted to explain or define tough words like "impedimenta" in paragraph 16, but, again, you don't have to. You're better off forcing them to deal with the fact that they'll sometimes see words they don't know.

The Questions

Let's look at some possible answers to these questions. We don't have choices, so your answers may vary. Note that for the sake of clarity the questions here are phrased slightly differently than they would be if they had answer choices. On the real test, questions are usually phrased as incomplete sentences that can be completed with the correct answer. Question 10, for example, would be written as "Jude responds to Mr. Philloston's departure with . . ."

Main Idea Question
1. *What happens in the passage?*

For fiction passages, instead of asking for the Main Idea or Purpose of the passage, questions will often simply ask what happens in the passage. Remember that we are not looking for a paragraph answer here. We want a *one-line summary*, enough to fit in an answer choice.

How about: **A boy says goodbye as a schoolteacher moves away.** That's all we need. Notice that we didn't even refer to the characters' names, a common occurrence for questions of this type.

Meaning Questions

2. *As it is used in paragraph 1, sentence 2, what does* effects *mean?*

For these questions, we must go back to the original sentence:

> *The miller at Cresscombe lent him the small white tilted cart and horse to carry his goods to the city of his destination, about twenty miles off, such a vehicle proving of quite sufficient size for the departing teacher's **effects**.*

Imagine the word in question wasn't there, just a blank, and we had to fill in that blank with another word. What word would we pick? Something like **belongings** would work.

3. *As it is used in paragraph 14, sentence 5, what does* afford *mean?*

Once again, let's go back to the sentence.

> *By going to live at Christminster, or near it, I shall be at headquarters, so to speak, and if my scheme is practicable at all, I consider that being on the spot will **afford** me a better chance of carrying it out than I should have elsewhere.*

What fits in that blank? Perhaps **provide**.

Explicit Questions

4. *According to the passage, why does Mr. Phillotson not take his piano with him?*

The answer to this is not tricky, but it may be tricky to know where to look. In this case, there are two reasons he's not taking the piano. First, paragraph 1 says he only has a small cart, so **it won't fit**. Second, paragraph 3 tells us that "even if he got it into the cart he should not know what to do with it on his arrival at Christminster, the city he was bound for, since he was only going into temporary lodgings just at first". So **he has nowhere to put it**.

5. *According to the passage, why is Mr. Phillotson moving away?*

Again, the hardest part is simply finding the answer (though here it might be a bit easier because we already read the most important lines in question 3 above). Try paragraph 14. There, Mr. Phillotson says he wants "to be a university graduate" and living in Christminster will make that easier. In short, **he's going to college**.

6. *How is Jude's reaction to Mr. Phillotson's departure different from that of the other students?*

The other students are mentioned in paragraph 8. While Jude is helping Mr. Phillotson pack his things, **the other boys do not help** and stand off to the side. The key here is to be sure not to read too much into the passage. We must stick to what it says. We don't know for sure why they do this (although we may have guesses). All we know for sure is what they do (or don't do).

Inferential Question

7. *Paragraph 2 suggests what about how the rector feels about Mr. Phillotson's departure?*

Now we have a question where we can't simply look up the answer. We have to deduce it based on what is written. Let's look at paragraph 2:

All paragraph 2 says about the rector's feelings is that he does not like change and that he therefore does not want to see the teacher leave. So he **considers the teacher's departure to be a significant change**. *Not* that he doesn't like the teacher, *not* that he's afraid, *not* that he likes the new teacher better. Any of those may well be true, but none are implied by the sentences in paragraph 2. Learning to make inferences also means learning not to infer *too much*.

Generalization Question

8. *Jude responds to Mr. Phillotson's departure with what emotion?*

For fiction passages, generalization questions often focus on the characters' emotional states. Here, we can see it right in paragraph 8: There are *tears* in his eyes. He is **sad** that his teacher is leaving. The real test will likely have more difficult choices than just "sadness", but starting this simple is a great first step toward getting to the right answer.

4

Writing Assignments

It may be tempting to spend less time on the essay in your preparation because it's optional and many colleges will not require it. That's understandable. However, *the act of preparing* for the essay helps strengthen skills that students will need on the English test. While the essay itself may not be as important, working on the essay can have multiplicative effects beyond the essay itself.

In this chapter, we will begin by briefly discussing the format of the essay. Then we will give several options for how to work the ACT essay into your classes, either as direct preparation for the ACT, or as a source for longer-term projects.

Format

We discussed this in Part I, but here's a refresher. Every essay prompt will begin with a brief discussion on a topic of general contemporary interest followed by three distinct perspectives on the topic. The "Essay Task" will always be the same:

> Write a unified, coherent essay in which you evaluate multiple perspectives on [the topic at hand]. In your essay, be sure to:
>
> ◆ Analyze and evaluate the perspectives given
> ◆ State and develop your own perspective on the issue
> ◆ Explain the relationship between your perspective and those given

The essay will be read by two readers, each giving the essay a score from 1 to 6 in four domains. The two scores are added together to give students a score from 2 to 12 in each domain:

- ◆ **Ideas and Analysis**. Do you address all three of the perspectives given? Do you understand the purpose of the essay? Do you take a clear position on the topic question? Do you offer context?
- ◆ **Development and Support**. Do you develop your ideas? Do you elaborate on your ideas?
- ◆ **Organization**. Is your essay well organized? Are your paragraphs related by a main idea? Are your transitions logical? Are your introduction and conclusion effective?
- ◆ **Language**. Do you show competent command of language? Do you show varied sentence structure? Do you make distracting errors?

The final Writing score is the rounded average of the four domain scores. Therefore, each domain contributes equally to the final Writing score. But that doesn't mean you have to spend equal time on all four domains. Depending on your students' particular strengths and weaknesses, some aspects may be easier to improve than others.

For our purposes, we'll mostly be talking about the domain scores rather than the final scaled score because it's an easier scale to comprehend and it's the scores that the readers are thinking about. What counts as a good score? For your purposes, a "good" score is one that is higher than where your students begin. A 4-4-4-4 is a good score if a student started with a 1-1-1-1, but not if they started with a 4-3-4-3. Like *all* ACT scores, because students might start from a wide range of scoring levels, it's best to think of them in terms of *improvement*, not in terms of absolute benchmarks.

Practice Tests

If your school is offering full-length practice tests, you should consider including the essay. Scheduling fully proctored tests can be very difficult; few schools have a spare 3 hours and 35 minutes lying around.

If you want to give a proctored test, but you're having trouble scheduling the time, you should consider skipping the essay. However, you can still give the essay separately at a different time. It's likely easier to find 40 minutes of free time; you can probably even do it during class.

It's certainly an option to assign essays as homework, but then you can't enforce the time limit. Timing on the redesigned essay is a bit more generous than timing on the old essay was, but timing still can be problem for some students. All practice tests produce more accurate scores (i.e., predictive of real test scores) when given under real test conditions. As such, it's best to give the essay as part of the full test; writing an essay in isolation is a different experience than writing one after having just sat through 3 hours of multiple choice sections. But timed sections in isolation are still better than untimed sections. If you can't find 40 straight minutes, don't break it up over multiple sessions; assign it for homework and have them time themselves. It's better for them to do it in one session, like on the real test, even if it is at home.

Additional Prompts

While full practice ACTs are plentiful, because the current essay format is new, there are only a handful of official ACT practice prompts available. The ACT's book, *The Official ACT Prep Guide*, contains three prompts with the three practice tests. There are two more available for free download on the ACT's website (one in the free test and one in the Sample Questions) plus another two in the paid online subscription course. That's a total of seven prompts, which should be plenty for most schools, but if you want proctored tests *and* in-class practice, you may want more.

It's actually not too hard to write your own prompts. All you need is some complex topic that does not have a simple yes or no answer. Here again is the prompt that we reprinted earlier along with the three perspectives:

It is now possible through genetic testing to determine an individual's likelihood of developing several different kinds of diseases, some of them debilitating or fatal. With such knowledge it may be possible for some people to seek early treatment or adopt lifestyle changes that may prevent or ameliorate these diseases. But others have no cure and no treatment or change in lifestyle will help. How much should we and do we want to know about our genetic disposition to disease? Should doctors tell patients? Who should have access to such information?

1. *The more we know about ourselves, the better. Even if we learn that we will eventually develop a fatal disease we deserve to know that and live our lives accordingly.*
2. *No science is exact, certainly not genetic testing. The possibility of inaccurate results is high. A false positive could destroy the life of a healthy person.*
3. *Our greatest concern should be individual privacy. It's easy to talk about doctor-patient confidentiality, but it is impossible to guarantee complete privacy.*

This may be a familiar topic, one that's been discussed in the media. It's also a kind of ethical question. You can probably think of similar issues off the top of your head, but you can find similar topics with a bit of rummaging around on the Internet:

◆ *To what extent should the government be responsible for reducing poverty?*
◆ *How do we balance environmental concerns with the requirements of modern life?*
◆ *What role should standardized testing have in high schools?*

You also want to make sure the topic is universal enough so that your students don't need specialized knowledge to address it. These kinds of topics can sometimes fall into areas that students have strong feelings about, so be mindful of this before walking into heated arguments in class.

The hardest part in writing a prompt may be coming up with three perspectives. We can see that the perspectives are more complex than a simple binary "genetic screening good" vs. "genetic screening bad". This is exactly the kind of nuance that the ACT is looking for and the reason they moved away from the old prompt, which did use such binary questions.

Of course, these don't have to be grand ethical questions. You can make them about anything you like, as long as you can find three unique perspectives on the issue.

Should schools institute dress codes?

◆ *Dress codes promote the kind of professionalism that students will later encounter in the workplace.*

◆ *Dress codes stifle individuality and creativity at a time when students are learning crucial social skills.*

◆ *Dress codes have benefits when applied fairly, but in practice they are often enforced with racial or gender biases.*

Seems like a lot of work? *Why not have the kids do it?*

This is an excellent exercise to have your students do. It might require a little bit of research, but not too much. We're not looking to actually write the essay (yet), we're just looking for topic ideas. Feel free to let them be creative and stray into wild territory, as long as they can come up with three distinct perspectives.

How to Score the Essay

A-List offers an essay scoring service for schools that use our online test assessment portal. If you want to give the essay as part of a full practice test, or if you simply have a lot of essays to grade, contact us to help you.

The alternative is to grade the essays yourself. The ACT, Inc. provides a scoring rubric for the essay in their book and on their website. Additionally, there are sample essays for the sample prompt given both in the book and on their website. Reviewing these essays can be very enlightening, particularly when compared with each other.

Ideally, student essays should be read by two people, each giving scores in the four domains. However, it may be difficult for you to enlist your colleagues to assist you. If you're the only one reading it, simply give the students one set of scores on the 6-point scale. Don't give scores on the 2- to 12-point scale. When people attempt that, they tend to start to make too fine a distinction: "Hmm, is this a 6 or a 7? It's kind of a 6½ . . ." Don't do that. An essay can't be "a 7". It can only be "a 3" or "a 4". If a student gets a 7, that just means two people disagree about whether it's a 3 or a 4.

Revision

The Domains

When grading, you're not obligated to give the same score in each domain. The whole point of having different grading categories is so you can evaluate the relative strengths and weaknesses of the essay instead of a holistic single number. To help sort it out, you can view the four domains as broadly split into two groups.

The Ideas and Analysis domain and the Development and Support domain together address how well you make your *argument*. How well do you choose your thesis? How well do you explain and address the perspectives? How well do you give explanations or examples to support your thesis?

The Organization domain and the Language domain are more about how well you actually *write*. How clear are your sentences? How unified are your paragraphs? Do you make transitions between them? Do you make mechanical errors?

You can work on improving Ideas and Analysis and Development and Support scores through group discussions without students writing a single word on the page. But the only way to improve Organization and Language scores is by writing. But simply writing over and over again won't make your writing any better. Students need to examine their essays to see how to improve them. If you don't change your habits, you won't change your scores.

You no doubt already do a fair share of writing work in your classes, so you don't need us to tell you how to discuss essays. But let's take some time to discuss how to treat the quirks of ACT essays.

In-Test Revision

During the test, students do have some opportunity for revision. With 40 minutes, students have a bit of a cushion such that they may be able to review their essays. They can't do major re-writes, but they can look it over, correct some careless spelling or grammatical errors, strike redundancies or add in a clarifying statement or two. (The readers know that this is a hand-written essay in a time limit, so it's totally fine to have ugly cross-outs or carets sticking words in the middle of sentences.)

After the test, you'll want to review the students' essays with them. This could be privately by writing comments on their essays (official test graders will not provide comments, only scores). It's often helpful to discuss essays publicly with the whole class, in order to demonstrate common problems that occur frequently. (If you do discuss student work publicly, you'll want to give students anonymity so they don't feel shamed about their weaknesses.) Having students work in small groups to workshop each other's essays can also be great, but you want to be sure they know what to look for. If every student in a group got a 1 on Language, there's no guarantee that teaming up will make their work any better.

If you'd prefer not to use real student essays, you can use the sample student essays from the ACT's book or website. They provide essays with scores ranging from 1 to 6. The downside is that each sample essay is given the same score across all four domains, so they aren't very helpful for students who are excelling in one domain but struggling in another.

The English Test

When reviewing and discussing these essays, you should do so in the framework *of the same categories tested on the English Test.* These categories are:

- **Usage/Mechanics**
    - *Grammar and Usage*: Grammar and relationships between words: verbs, pronouns, idioms
    - *Sentence Structure*: Relationships between clauses: run-ons, fragments, modifiers
    - *Punctuation*: Commas, colons, semicolons, periods
- **Rhetorical Skills**
    - *Style*: Word choice, tone, redundancy, conciseness, vagueness
    - *Organization*: Sequencing of sentences and paragraphs, transitions
    - *Strategy*: How your argument unfolds, adding or deleting sentences

The English Test is passage-based in order to mimic the act of editing an essay. So when you're *actually* editing an essay, you should be thinking about making the same kinds of changes you've seen on multiple-choice writing questions.

Do this *explicitly*. If you prepare a student essay to discuss in front of the class, take note of the kinds of problems you found in it. Then go find English questions that test the same errors, such as subject-verb agreement, redundant expressions, vague language, improper transition words, and many more. This way, you can prepare for the essay and the English Test at the same time. It reinforces the idea that the things you're asked on the multiple-choice questions aren't arbitrary annoyances—they're the things you do to make your writing better. The act of reviewing the essay strengthens the rules you discussed for the English Test.

It's important to note that all six of these categories are important. Teachers often get pulled too much in only one direction. Some spend all their time talking about content and development. That's great—that affects your Writing scores too. But it's meaningless if your language is unidiomatic to the point of non-fluency. Others spend all their time circling commas and pronouns and spelling errors. That's great—sloppy writing obscures your argument. But you also want to make sure the argument makes sense.

A New Draft

It's fun to review and discuss essays (well, maybe not fun, but useful), but why not go further and *have students actually rewrite their essays*. Make it a homework assignment so they can take their time with it. Have them take their notes from the classroom discussion and apply it to their own work to make it better.

These edits should not be drastic. Students shouldn't entirely re-write the essay from scratch. Don't add five more paragraphs. (But do feel free to split your one-long-paragraph essay into five coherent paragraphs.) You can place limits on what they do to ensure it's a revision, for example, page limits or requiring a certain amount of the original essay remains unchanged. Don't write a new essay, just make what you already have better. It could be purely a revision based on the language and rhetoric of their own arguments, depending on which skills you want to focus on.

Obviously this task is outside of the scope of the ACT. Once those 40 minutes are up, the essays are done. If a student got a 2 Language score when timed and later revised it into a 4 Language score, that doesn't mean he or she will be able to get a 4 on the first try during a timed section. But the fact that they can push it up to a 4 means it's *possible*. Some kids literally have no idea what good writing looks like. Getting them to recognize the difference between good and bad writing is valuable in its own right. And it can be a big confidence boost for them to know that they are capable of producing good writing.

Expand the Assignment

As we saw in Part II, several of the Common Core Standards do not align with the ACT essay because the standards require more extensive writing than a single 40-minute essay allows. However, if these standards are important to your class, you can stretch ACT essay prompts to longer and more ambitious assignments.

Research to Build and Present Knowledge

Writing standards 7, 8, and 9 focus on research, obviously outside the scope of the 40-minute ACT essay. But the essay prompts are great jumping off points for research projects.

We already discussed the kinds of topics that are used for the prompt as well as how to come up with your own prompts. As we can see, these are all topics that can be fertile ground for additional discussion beyond the four-page essay.

First of all, have students look for actual sources that address the issue. Additional sources can be of a variety of types. Some may be more objective reporting to give the historical context of the topic: what is the situation, how has it arisen, why is anyone talking about this. But it's also important to find more *opinions* on the issue. Perspective 1 says intelligent machines make us lose our humanity? Try to find an article that actually argues this point. Try to find real-life examples of people arguing each of the three perspectives.

You don't have to restrict yourself to news media either. Literature is often fertile territory for discussion of grand ethical topics. Writing about the dangers of intelligent machines making us lose our humanity? Why not read some Philip K. Dick novels? Don't limit yourself to print. Maybe let them write about films, as well.

Production and Distribution of Writing

Writing standards 4, 5, and 6 are about the production and distribution of writing. Standards 4 and 5 we've already addressed: the former is about the production of writing and the latter about revision. Standard 6 is about the use of technology in writing. Again, that's outside the scope of the 40-minute ACT essay, but easily within the scope of an extended research project.

First of all, if the students are doing research at all, chances are they'll be using the Internet. Hopefully they'll go beyond googling the topic and clicking on the first link that mentions it. If they don't, that's something you can work on with them: how to do more extensive and effective research. You don't have to roam the basement halls of a library's periodical room, but you do have to go beyond Wikipedia.

Second, they can use technology in their actual writing. Standard 6 mentions using the Internet for publishing and collaboration, something you can definitely have your students do. Instead of individual projects, assign these research tasks to teams. Have them set up webpages to discuss their findings and come up with new perspectives. Log these conversations so you can see how their theses develop.

Third, they can incorporate multimedia elements into their final presentations. Did your students find any data or statistics supporting any of the perspectives? Find the source of those figures. Make a table or graph showing those numbers. Or make representations of other numbers you find in your research.

Range of Writing

Standard 10 emphasized writing "routinely over extended time frames (time for research, reflection, and revision) and shorter time frames (a single sitting or a day or two) for a range of tasks, purposes, and audiences". That's certainly applicable to the kind of research project we describe here. We start with a short-term project like the actual ACT essay prompt. We adapt that essay with reflection and revision through several drafts. Then we expand the task into a larger research project or presentation that could stretch over several weeks. You could even stretch the assignment over the entire semester, if you like. The topic is pliable enough to be slipped into whatever time frame you have available.

Essay Assignment Summary

I. Basic Practice and Revision

1. Pick a topic to assign.
   a. It could be a real ACT prompt.
   b. Or you can have students write their own prompts.
2. Have students write a one- to four-page essay about the passage according to the standard ACT prompt.
   a. Ideally this will be as part of a full-practice test.
   b. If not, try to administer it separately in a timed 40-minute session.
   c. If that's not possible, assign it for homework.
3. Grade the essays, either by yourself, with a colleague, or using A-List.
4. Discuss essays with the students. There are several ways you could do this:
   a. Give individual comments on students' essays.
   b. Discuss anonymized student essays with the entire class.
   c. Discuss the ACT, Inc.'s sample student essays with the entire class.
   d. Have students workshop each other's essays together in small groups.
5. When discussing essays, do so in the context of the English Test categories:
   a. Grammar and Usage
   b. Sentence Structure
   c. Punctuation
   d. Style
   e. Organization
   f. Writing Strategy
6. Have students use notes to revise their essays.
7. Regrade the essays and give feedback about what's improved.

II. Extended Research

1. Choose an ACT prompt to your liking. It can be one they've already written about, but it doesn't have to be.

2. Have students research additional sources on the same topic discussed in the prompt and build a writing assignment around it.
   a. Find sources that argue the same points as the three perspectives.
   b. Look for historical background and write about the context of the issue.
   c. Use fiction, literary, or other media sources.
3. Use technology in research and writing production.
   a. Use the Internet for research (effectively!).
   b. Use the Internet to collaborate with other students and log conversations.
   c. Use multimedia sources to supplement the project with tables, graphs, and other figures.
4. Extend this project over whatever time period you have available, from a multipage paper to a longer in-class presentation.

Appendix
All ELA Alignment Tables

How to Read the Tables

Each Anchor Standard is shown in a table followed by the grade-specific standard for grades 11–12. Each table contains columns showing:

- The code for the standard, as defined by the CCSSI
- The standard itself
- Its alignment with the ACT

Each standard has a code containing three parts: letters denoting the strand or content area, the grade level of the standard or "CCR" for Anchor Standards, and the sequential number of the standard (sometimes with letters for subpoints). For example, "RL.CCR.5" refers to the fifth Anchor Standard in the Reading Literature strand, and "W.11-12.3a" refers to the first subskill of the third standard for the grade 11–12 standard in the Writing strand.

The two alignment columns will each display one of the following symbols:

- **Y** = The standard is aligned with the ACT.
- **N** = The standard is not aligned with the ACT.
- **P** = The standard is partially aligned with ACT. This means a qualifying comment was listed for the standard in the original alignment document.

Reading CCR Anchor Standards

Code	Standard	Aligns
Key Ideas and Details		
R.CCR.1	Read closely to determine what the text says explicitly and to make logical inferences from it; cite specific textual evidence when writing or speaking to support conclusions drawn from the text.	**P**
R.CCR.2	Determine central ideas or themes of a text and analyze their development; summarize the key supporting details and ideas.	**Y**
R.CCR.3	Analyze how and why individuals, events, and ideas develop and interact over the course of a text.	**Y**
Craft and Structure		
R.CCR.4	Interpret words and phrases as they are used in a text, including determining technical, connotative, and figurative meanings, and analyze how specific word choices shape meaning or tone.	**Y**
R.CCR.5	Analyze the structure of texts, including how specific sentences, paragraphs, and larger portions of the text (e.g., a section, chapter, scene, or stanza) relate to each other and the whole.	**Y**
R.CCR.6	Assess how point of view or purpose shapes the content and style of a text.	**Y**
Integration of Knowledge and Ideas		
R.CCR.7	Integrate and evaluate content presented in diverse formats and media, including visually and quantitatively, as well as in words.	**PS**
R.CCR.8	Delineate and evaluate the argument and specific claims in a text, including the validity of the reasoning as well as the relevance and sufficiency of the evidence.	**YRS**
R.CCR.9	Analyze how two or more texts address similar themes or topics in order to build knowledge or to compare the approaches the authors take.	**YRS**
Range of Reading and Level of Text Complexity		
R.CCR.10	Read and comprehend complex literary and informational texts independently and proficiently.	**Y**

Reading Standards for Literature

Code	Standard	Aligns
Key Ideas and Details		
RL.11-12.1	Cite strong and thorough textual evidence to support analysis of what the text says explicitly as well as inferences drawn from the text, including determining where the text leaves matters uncertain.	**N**
RL.11-12.2	Determine two or more themes or central ideas of a text and analyze their development over the course of the text, including how they interact and build on one another to produce a complex account; provide an objective summary of the text.	**P**
RL.11-12.3	Analyze the impact of the author's choices regarding how to develop and relate elements of a story or drama (e.g., where a story is set, how the action is ordered, how the characters are introduced and developed).	**P**
Craft and Structure		
RL.11-12.4	Determine the meaning of words and phrases as they are used in the text, including figurative and connotative meanings; analyze the impact of specific word choices on meaning and tone, including words with multiple meanings or language that is particularly fresh, engaging, or beautiful. (Include Shakespeare as well as other authors.)	**P**
RL.11-12.5	Analyze how an author's choices concerning how to structure specific parts of a text (e.g., the choice of where to begin or end a story, the choice to provide a comedic or tragic resolution) contribute to its overall structure and meaning as well as its aesthetic impact.	**Y**
RL.11-12.6	Analyze a case in which grasping point of view requires distinguishing what is directly stated in a text from what is really meant (e.g., satire, sarcasm, irony, or understatement).	**Y**
Integration of Knowledge and Ideas		
RL.11-12.7	Analyze multiple interpretations of a story, drama, or poem (e.g., recorded or live production of a play or recorded novel or poetry), evaluating how each version interprets the source text. (Include at least one play by Shakespeare and one play by an American dramatist.)	**N**
RL.11-12.8	(Not applicable to literature)	–

(Continued)

Code	Standard	Aligns
RL.11-12.9	Demonstrate knowledge of eighteenth-, nineteenth- and early-twentieth-century foundational works of American literature, including how two or more texts from the same period treat similar themes or topics.	N

Range of Reading and Level of Text Complexity

Code	Standard	Aligns
RL.11-12.10	By the end of grade 11, read and comprehend literature, including stories, dramas, and poems, in the grades 11–CCR text complexity band proficiently, with scaffolding as needed at the high end of the range. By the end of grade 12, read and comprehend literature, including stories, dramas, and poems, at the high end of the grades 11–CCR text complexity band independently and proficiently	P

Reading Standards for Informational Text

Code	Standard	Aligns
Key Ideas and Details		
RI.11-12.1	Cite strong and thorough textual evidence to support analysis of what the text says explicitly as well as inferences drawn from the text, including determining where the text leaves matters uncertain.	N
RI.11-12.2	Determine two or more central ideas of a text and analyze their development over the course of the text, including how they interact and build on one another to provide a complex analysis; provide an objective summary of the text.	P
RI.11-12.3	Analyze a complex set of ideas or sequence of events and explain how specific individuals, ideas, or events interact and develop over the course of the text.	Y
Craft and Structure		
RI.11-12.4	Determine the meaning of words and phrases as they are used in a text, including figurative, connotative, and technical meanings; analyze how an author uses and refines the meaning of a key term or terms over the course of a text (e.g., how Madison defines faction in Federalist No. 10).	Y
RI.11-12.5	Analyze and evaluate the effectiveness of the structure an author uses in his or her exposition or argument, including whether the structure makes points clear, convincing, and engaging.	P
RI.11-12.6	Determine an author's point of view or purpose in a text in which the rhetoric is particularly effective, analyzing how style and content contribute to the power, persuasiveness, or beauty of the text.	N
Integration of Knowledge and Ideas		
RI.11-12.7	Integrate and evaluate multiple sources of information presented in different media or formats (e.g., visually, quantitatively) as well as in words in order to address a question or solve a problem.	PS
RI.11-12.8	Delineate and evaluate the reasoning in seminal U.S. texts, including the application of constitutional principles and use of legal reasoning (e.g., in U.S. Supreme Court majority opinions and dissents) and the premises, purposes, and arguments in works of public advocacy (e.g., The Federalist, presidential addresses).	N

(Continued)

Code	Standard	Aligns
RI.11-12.9	Analyze seventeenth-, eighteenth-, and nineteenth-century foundational U.S. documents of historical and literary significance (including The Declaration of Independence, the Preamble to the Constitution, the Bill of Rights, and Lincoln's Second Inaugural Address) for their themes, purposes, and rhetorical features.	N

Range of Reading and Level of Text Complexity

Code	Standard	Aligns
RI.11-12.10	By the end of grade 11, read and comprehend literary nonfiction in the grades 11–CCR text complexity band proficiently, with scaffolding as needed at the high end of the range. By the end of grade 12, read and comprehend literary nonfiction at the high end of the grades 11–CCR text complexity band independently and proficiently.	Y

Writing CCR Anchor Standards

Code	Standard	Aligns
Text Types and Purposes		
W.CCR.1	Write arguments to support claims in an analysis of substantive topics or texts, using valid reasoning and relevant and sufficient evidence.	**P**
W.CCR.2	Write informative/explanatory texts to examine and convey complex ideas and information clearly and accurately through the effective selection, organization, and analysis of content.	**Y**
W.CCR.3	Write narratives to develop real or imagined experiences or events using effective technique, well-chosen details, and well-structured event sequences.	**N**
Production and Distribution of Writing		
W.CCR.4	Produce clear and coherent writing in which the development, organization, and style are appropriate to task, purpose, and audience.	**P**
W.CCR.5	Develop and strengthen writing as needed by planning, revising, editing, rewriting, or trying a new approach.	**PE**
W.CCR.6	Use technology, including the Internet, to produce and publish writing and to interact and collaborate with others.	**N**
Research to Build and Present Knowledge		
W.CCR.7	Conduct short as well as more sustained research projects based on focused questions, demonstrating understanding of the subject under investigation.	**N**
W.CCR.8	Gather relevant information from multiple print and digital sources, assess the credibility and accuracy of each source, and integrate the information while avoiding plagiarism.	**N**
W.CCR.9	Draw evidence from literary or informational texts to support analysis, reflection, and research.	**N**
Range of Writing		
W.CCR.10	Write routinely over extended time frames (time for research, reflection, and revision) and shorter time frames (a single sitting or a day or two) for a range of tasks, purposes, and audiences.	**P**

Writing Grades 11–12 Standards

Code	Standard	Aligns
Text Types and Purposes		
W.11-12.1a	Introduce precise, knowledgeable claim(s), establish the significance of the claim(s), distinguish the claim(s) from alternate or opposing claim(s), counterclaims, reasons, and evidence.	**Y**
W.11-12.1b	Develop claim(s) and counterclaims fairly and thoroughly, supplying the most relevant evidence for each while pointing out the strengths and limitations of both in a manner that anticipates the audience's knowledge level, concerns, values, and possible biases.	**Y**
W.11-12.1c	Use words, phrases, and clauses as well as varied syntax to link the major sections of the text, create cohesion, and clarify the relationships between claim(s) and reasons, between reasons and evidence, and between claim(s) and counterclaims.	**P**
W.11-12.1d	Establish and maintain a formal style and objective tone while attending to the norms and conventions of the discipline in which they are writing.	**N**
W.11-12.1e	Provide a concluding statement or section that follows from and supports the argument presented.	**P**
W.11-12.2a	Introduce a topic; organize complex ideas, concepts, and information so that each new element builds on that which preceded it to create a unified whole; include formatting (e.g., headings), graphics (e.g., figures, tables), and multimedia when useful to aiding comprehension.	**P**
W.11-12.2b	Develop the topic thoroughly by selecting the most significant and relevant facts, extended definitions, concrete details, quotations, or other information and examples appropriate to the audience's knowledge of the topic.	**Y**
W.11-12.2c	Use appropriate and varied transitions and syntax to link the major sections of the text, create cohesion, and clarify the relationships among complex ideas and concepts.	**P**
W.11-12.2d	Use precise language, domain-specific vocabulary, and techniques such as metaphor, simile, and analogy to manage the complexity of the topic.	**Y**
W.11-12.2e	Establish and maintain a formal style and objective tone while attending to the norms and conventions of the discipline in which they are writing.	**N**

Code	Standard	Aligns
W.11-12.2f	Provide a concluding statement or section that follows from and supports the argument presented (e.g., articulating implications or the significance of the topic).	**P**
W.11-12.3a	Engage and orient the reader by setting out a problem, situation, or observation and its significance, establishing one or multiple point(s) of view, and introducing a narrator and/or characters; create a smooth progression of experiences or events.	**N**
W.11-12.3b	Use narrative techniques, such as dialogue, pacing, description, reflection, and multiple plot lines, to develop experiences, events, and/or characters.	**N**
W.11-12.3c	Use a variety of techniques to sequence events so that they build on one another to create a coherent whole and build toward a particular tone and outcome (e.g., a sense of mystery, suspense, growth, or resolution).	**N**
W.11-12.3d	Use precise words and phrases, telling details, and sensory language to convey a vivid picture of the experiences, events, setting, and/or characters.	**N**
W.11-12.3e	Provide a conclusion that follows from and reflects on what is experienced, observed, or resolved over the course of the narrative.	**N**

Production and Distribution of Writing

Code	Standard	Aligns
W.11-12.4	(Grade-specific expectations for writing types are defined in standards 1–3.)	–
W.11-12.5	Develop and strengthen writing as needed by planning, revising, editing, rewriting, or trying a new approach, focusing on addressing what is most significant for a specific purpose and audience. (Editing for conventions should demonstrate command of Language standards 1–3 up to and including grades 11–12).	**PE**
W.11-12.6	Use technology, including the Internet, to produce, publish and update individual or share writing products in response to ongoing feedback, including new arguments or information.	**N**

Research to Build and Present Knowledge

Code	Standard	Aligns
W.11-12.7	Conduct short as well as more sustained research projects to answer a question (including a self-generated question) or solve a problem, narrow or broaden the inquiry when appropriate; synthesize multiple sources on the subject, demonstrating understanding of the subject under investigation.	**N**

(Continued)

Code	Standard	Aligns
W.11-12.8	Gather relevant information from multiple authoritative print and digital sources, using advanced searches effectively; assess the strengths and limitations of each source in terms of the task, purpose, and audience; integrate the information into the text selectively to maintain the flow of ideas, avoiding plagiarism and overreliance on any one source and following a standard format for citation.	**N**
W.11-12.9a	Apply grades 11–12 Reading standards to literature (e.g., "Demonstrate knowledge of eighteenth-, nineteenth-, and early-twentieth-century foundational works of American literature, including how two or more texts from the same period treat similar themes or topics").	**N**
W.11-12.9b	Apply grades 11–12 Reading standards to literary nonfiction (e.g., "Delineate and evaluate the reasoning in seminal U.S. texts, including the application of constitutional principles and use of legal reasoning [e.g., in U.S. Supreme Court Case majority opinions and dissents] and the premises, purposes, and arguments in works of public advocacy [e.g., The Federalist, presidential addresses]").	**N**

Range of Writing

Code	Standard	Aligns
W.11-12.10	Write routinely over extended time frames (time for research, reflection, and revision) and shorter time frames (a single sitting or a day or two) for a range of tasks, purposes, and audiences.	**P**

Language CCR Anchor Standards

Code	Standard	Aligns
Conventions of Standard English		
L.CCR.1	Demonstrate command of the conventions of standard English grammar and usage when writing or speaking.	**PEW**
L.CCR.2	Demonstrate command of the conventions of standard English capitalization, punctuation, and spelling when writing.	**PEW**
Knowledge of Language		
L.CCR.3	Apply knowledge of language to understand how language functions in different contexts, to make effective choices for meaning or style, and to comprehend more fully when reading or listening.	**PERW**
Vocabulary Acquisition and Use		
L.CCR.4	Determine or clarify the meaning of unknown and multiple-meaning words and phrases by using context clues, analyzing meaningful word parts, and consulting general and specialized reference materials, as appropriate.	**PR**
L.CCR.5	Demonstrate understanding of figurative language, word relationships, and nuances in word meanings.	**YR**
L.CCR.6	Acquire and use accurately a range of general academic and domain-specific words and phrases sufficient for reading, writing, speaking, and listening at the college and career readiness level; demonstrate independence in gathering vocabulary knowledge when considering a word or phrase important to comprehension or expression.	**PERWS**

Language Grades 11–12 Standards

Code	Standard	Aligns
Conventions of Standard English		
L.11-12.1a	Apply the understanding that usage is a matter of convention, can change over time, and is sometimes contested.	**PEW**
L.11-12.1b	Resolve issues of complex or contested usage, consulting references (e.g., *Merriam-Webster's Dictionary of English Usage, Garner's Modern American Usage*) as needed.	**N**
L.11-12.2a	Observe hyphenation conventions.	**N**
L.11-12.2b	Spell correctly.	**N**
Knowledge of Language		
L.11-12.3a	Vary syntax for effect, consulting references (e.g., Tufte's Artful Sentences) for guidance as needed; apply an understanding of syntax to the study of complex tasks when reading.	**PRW**
Vocabulary Acquisition and Use		
L.11-12.4	Determine or clarify the meaning of unknown and multiple-meaning words and phrases based on grades 11–12 reading and content, choosing flexibly from a range of strategies.	**PR**
L.11-12.4a	Use context (e.g., the overall meaning of a sentence, paragraph, or text; a word's position or function in a sentence) as a clue to the meaning of a word or phrase.	**YR**
L.11-12.4b	Identify and correctly use patterns of word changes that indicate different meanings or parts of speech (e.g., conceive, conception, conceivable).	**YE**
L.11-12.4c	Consult general and specialized reference materials (e.g., dictionaries, glossaries, thesauruses), both print and digital, to find the pronunciation of a word or determine or clarify its precise meaning, its part of speech, its etymology, or its standard usage.	**N**
L.11-12.4d	Verify the preliminary determination of the meaning of a word or phrase (e.g., by checking the inferred meaning in context or in a dictionary).	**N**
L.11-12.5a	Interpret figures of speech (e.g., hyperbole, paradox) in context and analyze their role in the text.	**YR**

Code	Standard	Aligns
L.11-12.5b	Analyze nuances in the meaning of words with similar denotations.	**YR**
L.11-12.6	Acquire and use accurately a range of general academic and domain-specific words and phrases sufficient for reading, writing, speaking, and listening at the college and career readiness level; demonstrate independence in gathering vocabulary knowledge when considering a word or phrase important to comprehension or expression.	**PERWS**

Progressive Skills

Code	Skill	Aligns
L.3.1f	Ensure subject-verb and pronoun-antecedent agreement.	Y
L.3.3a	Choose words and phrases for effect.	Y
L.4.1f	Produce complete sentences, recognizing and correcting inappropriate fragments and run-ons.	Y
L.4.1g	Correctly use frequently confused words (e.g., to/too/ two; there/their).	Y
L.4.3a	Choose words and phrases to convey ideas precisely. (Subsumed by L.7.3a)	–
L.4.3b	Choose punctuation for effect.	Y
L.5.1d	Recognize and correct inappropriate shifts in verb tense.	Y
L.5.2a	Use punctuation to separate items in a series (subsumed by L.9-10.1a).	Y
L.6.1c	Recognize and correct inappropriate shifts in pronoun number and person.	Y
L.6.1d	Recognize and correct vague pronouns (i.e., ones with unclear or ambiguous antecedents).	Y
L.6.1e	Recognize variations from standard English in their own and others' writing and speaking, and identify and use strategies to improve expression in conventional language.	P
L.6.2a	Use punctuation (commas, parentheses, dashes) to set off nonrestrictive/parenthetical elements.	Y
L.6.3a	Vary sentence patters for meaning, reader/listener interest, and style (subsumed by L.11-12.3a).	Y
L.6.3b	Maintain consistency in style and tone.	Y
L.7.1c	Place phrases and clauses within a sentence, recognizing and correcting misplaced and dangling modifiers.	Y
L.7.3a	Choose language that expresses ideas precisely and concisely, recognizing and eliminating wordiness and redundancy.	Y
L.8.1d	Recognize and correct inappropriate shifts in verb voice and mood.	Y
L.9-10.1a	Use parallel structure.	Y

Additional Resources

A-List

Main website: www.alisteducation.com
Bookstore: www.alisteducation.com/bookstore

The ACT

Main websites:
    www.act.org
    www.actstudent.org
The Alignment of Common Core and ACT's College and Career Readiness System, ACT, Inc., June 2010. [No longer posted on act.org]
The Official ACT Prep Guide, 2016–2017, Wiley, 2016.
An ACT, Inc., book that contains three full-length practice ACTs.
The Real ACT Prep Guide, 3rd Edition, Peterson's, 2011.
An earlier version of the book that contains five full-length practice ACTs. There is some overlap between the material in these tests and the material in the tests in *The Official ACT Prep Guide*. Note Wiley produced a 2016 printing of the same book. Be sure to pay attention to the titles when ordering books.
Preparing for the ACT 2015–2016, free booklet containing a full practice test:
    www.act.org/content/dam/act/unsecured/documents/
    Preparing-for-the-ACT.pdf
Practice test booklet order form:
    www.act.org/content/dam/act/unsecured/documents/
    ACT-SampleTestBookOrderForm.pdf
ACT College and Career Readiness Standards:
    www.act.org/content/act/en/education-and-career-planning/
    CollegeandCareerReadinessStandards.html

The Common Core State Standards

Main website:
    www.corestandards.org
The Standards (available to read on the web or as pdf downloads):
    www.corestandards.org/the-standards